a mothercare book

UNDERSTANDING YOUR CHILD THROUGH PLAY

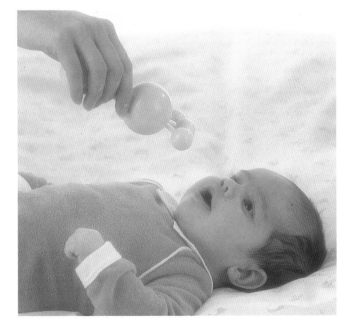

MAGGIE JONES

INTRODUCTION BY DAVID ELKIND, Ph.D.

ILLUSTRATIONS BY SHELAGH McNICHOLAS

PRENTICE
HALL
PRESS

New York London Toronto Sydney Tokyo

CONTENTS

Here goes

2–3 YEARS

52

Taking off

3–5 YEARS

70

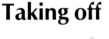

PRENTICE HALL PRESS
15 Columbus Circle
New York, NY 10023

Originally published in Great Britain by
Conran Octopus Limited,
37 Shelton Street, London WC2H 9HN

PRENTICE HALL PRESS and colophon are
registered trademarks of
Simon & Schuster, Inc.

Library of Congress Cataloging-in-Publication
Data

Jones, Maggie.
  Understanding your child through play.

  "First published in 1989 by Conran Octopus
Limited" – P.
  1. Play – Psychological aspects.   2. Child
psychology.   I. Title
BF717.J65 1990   649'.5   89–23120

ISBN 0–13–932906–4

Designed by Louise Bruce

Manufactured by Mandarin, Hong Kong

10 9 8 7 6 5 4 3 2 1

First Prentice Hall Press Edition

INTRODUCTION

Play is the activity by which the infant or young child learns about herself and about the world. Because both the self and the world are so new, a child is constantly learning, and thus continuously playing. For the infant and young child, play is not a frivolous activity, but rather the most adaptive practice a child can engage in.

It is this very special insight as to the central role of play in the life of the infant and young child that informs this book. As parents, we may accept the importance of play without knowing where to go with that idea. The author shows us. She provides a wealth of ideas for playing with infants and young children that we could hardly have come up with on our own. The richness of the suggestions gives us many different options and allows us to choose the play activities that we personally find most congenial. For example, of the several songs she suggests we might sing to the child, I would feel most comfortable singing "My Bonnie Lies over the Ocean." The point is that we sing to the child and that we sing something that we enjoy singing.

Moreover, the author provides activities that speak to all facets of the child's growing awareness of self and world. There are play activities to enrich the child's visual world, as well as the worlds of touch, taste, sound and movement. There are play activities for each successive age of development together with suggested age levels. A special fringe benefit is that many of the activities require nothing more than what is readily available in most homes. There are, however, also excellent guidelines for toy selection.

I believe this is a most helpful and balanced book for parents. It provides a wealth of innovative ideas for enriching the child's experience at the same time that they strengthen the relationship between child and caregiver. And the activities are nicely geared to general principles of development while leaving plenty of room for individual differences in rate of growth.

David Elkind, Ph.D.
Professor of Child Study, Tufts University
Author of MISEDUCATION: PRESCHOOLERS AT RISK

First toys

From the beginning your new baby is a person with a potential to learn and play. He is very aware of his environment from birth and responds to brightly-colored moving objects, to sounds, and above all to the human face and voice. Right from the start your baby can see, hear and feel and he is learning all the time, so don't miss out on this opportunity to enjoy being with him and to help him make sense of his surroundings. Although your new baby may sleep a great deal at first, most soon spend periods awake in which they are neither feeding nor crying, and these times provide a chance for you to get to know your baby, talk to him, cuddle him, and introduce him to the new world around him. Provide him with bright mobiles and pictures to look at, give him things to feel and grasp with his hands and talk and sing to him. Your baby may cry for reasons other than hunger or discomfort and needs you to pick him up, cuddle and play with him. He is happier if he is stimulated and will be getting the encouragement he needs to make the most of his growing abilities. Above all, enjoy your baby; he learns more from you than from any toys.

Looking around

When he is first put into your arms your baby may look up at you and study your face intently. Many newborn babies are surprisingly alert. At first, a newborn baby is most attracted by bright colors and strong patterns, especially by the pattern of the human face. He can focus best on objects which are held at 8–10in (20–25cm) from his face. This is about the distance where you would probably naturally hold him when looking and talking to him. Take time over these early 'conversations', touching his nose, cheeks, fingers and toes. You may feel awkward at first but smiling and cooing will soon come naturally, particularly as you get used to each other and your baby becomes even more responsive. Even a tiny baby tries to mirror the expression

You can hang a mobile above your baby's crib or changing table or anywhere he spends some time.

he sees, raising his eyebrows or sticking out his tongue.

Something to see
A mobile makes an ideal first amusement. Choose one with bright colors which moves easily – either a lightweight one which will swing in the slightest breeze or perhaps a musical one which winds up and runs for some time. It should be

Pictures inside your baby's crib provide him with interesting things to look at during wakeful moments. Faces cut out of magazines, postcards, a paper plate with a clown face drawn on it, pictures from a board book, or a small plastic safety mirror can be put in and changed often so that your baby has new things to look at.

close enough for him to see it or you may need to hold him up so that he can watch it.

At first you can hang mobiles within your baby's range of vision but when he begins to swipe at objects within his reach, a fragile mobile may have to be moved.

However, you may find that hanging an object to swipe at above your baby's carriage or crib provides new amusement. This can be any simple object – a soft ball, a rattle, a piece of colored cardboard. Before he starts to try to grasp things, remove anything that might be harmful if he got it in his mouth, and perhaps buy or make a baby gym – a string of brightly-colored objects to stretch across the crib which he can swing at, grab hold of and make a noise with.

New babies spend a lot of their day lying in their carriage, cradle or crib. While most of that time they are asleep, some like to spend short, quiet periods awake – some amusing themselves by watching their moving hands, or looking at the pattern of the covers or lining of the crib. Your baby probably won't be happy to lie awake for long in his crib or cradle and will need your company whether he is fretful or not. He will look up at your eyes and study your face, enjoy your talking and singing to him and practice his early smiles.

Brightly-colored objects
Even a young baby may be interested in rattles and other objects, especially those that are brightly colored. From early on he can follow the

movement a little way backwards and forwards if you slowly pass the rattle in front of his eyes. Objects don't have to make a noise to attract his attention. At first a baby's hands are usually held closed in little fists, but gradually he will relax them – if you put an object into his open palm he will close his hand around it. However, he will have no control over what he does with it so often it will quickly be released. At this age it is better just to concentrate on showing him things. By the age of two or three months he may be reaching out and trying to touch things. These are important early steps towards learning to coordinate his hand movements with his eye. This is a skill he starts to practice now, though he won't be able to grasp anything properly yet. Although babies are born with a very strong grasp reflex, this soon disappears and your baby will need to learn to hold things all over again.

At two or three months your baby will probably be ready to spend more time sitting in a bouncing cradle. In this

Random hand movements become more deliberate and accurate as hand-eye coordination improves.

position he can look "out" on the world and is also freer to use his hands. This is when a toy fixed across the front of the cradle begins to come into its own. He will at first make random movements with his hands and occasionally succeed in hitting the toy and making it move. This excites him to do more. Gradually his movements become more deliberate and he sees that he can make something happen.

Home made mobiles
Mobiles that you make yourself can be infinitely variable. They are easily made by hanging a variety of bright objects from a coat hanger. Crinkly foil, pictures cut out of magazines, and brightly-colored shapes will all attract your baby's eye.

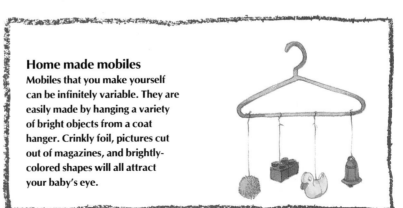

Sound and music

Many parents notice fleeting smiles or half smiles from birth, but from about six weeks your baby probably responds to your voice and looks into your eyes with his first really sustained, delightful smiles.

A newborn baby is very aware of sounds. A baby can hear while in the womb and after birth quickly recognizes his mother's voice. A new baby will be especially attracted by the sound of your voice, so it is never too early to start talking and singing to him because this is essential for listening, understanding and his own speech later. Some babies like their surroundings to be very quiet and peaceful, others like to have some background noise. Some babies respond well to the lullaby tapes which imitate the sounds inside the womb, especially if these are played within six weeks of the birth. They are less successful after this time since the baby seems to have forgotten the sounds and the effect is lost.

Speaking and singing
Most of all, though, a young baby responds to voices – parents, sisters, brothers, grandparents and others. When he is alert, but not hungry, you will want to hold him on your lap and talk and sing to him; he needs this kind of attention just as he needs food and warmth. A little later, he will begin to echo little cooing sounds back at you. You can keep up a kind of "conversation" for some time; you saying something, then waiting till he makes a sound back. You may instinctively make exaggerated faces and use cooing speech when you talk to him. Remember that a baby's responses are quite slow, and give him plenty of time to "talk" back to you. These "conversations" are essential for learning about taking turns, listening and copying – all part of communicating.

Most small babies will like the sound of your singing. It doesn't matter what songs you sing, but lullabies and nursery rhyme songs remain favorites. Many records and tapes are available to remind you of the words and melodies. At this

Songs to sing

My bonnie lies over the ocean
My bonnie lies over the sea
My bonnie lies over the ocean
So bring back my bonnie to me.
Bring back, bring back, oh
bring back my bonnie to me,
to me,
Bring back, bring back, oh
bring back my bonnie to me.

Dance for your daddy
My little laddy
Dance for your daddy
My little man.
You shall have a fishy
In a little dishy
You shall have a fishy
When his boat comes in.

Mama's little baby likes
short'ning, short'ning
Mama's little baby likes
short'ning bread.
(Repeat)

We took him to the doctor an'
the doctor he said:
Mama's little baby likes
short'ning bread.
(Repeat first verse)

stage, though, the most important thing is contact. *What* you sing or say to your child is not so important as taking the time to communicate with him.

Following sounds

Many early toys make sounds to attract the baby's attention and eyes to an object. Rattles, squeaky toys, musical mobiles or music boxes all arouse his interest. Later, when he begins to make more purposeful movements with his hands, he will be fascinated when he touches an object and it makes a sound.

If you watch your baby's eyes you will notice that he may show he is listening by searching for a sound with his eyes. A game he can play to help him to find the source of a noise and to begin to notice

that he can make something happen is "musical mittens." Take a pair of brightly-colored mittens and sew a little bell onto each. He will soon discover that when he waves his hand, it makes a noise. You can put one mitten on one hand first, then on the other,

Mittens that make a noise, rattles, music boxes and wind chimes may all attract your baby's attention.

then on both hands. Remember not to leave him unattended with the mittens on in case he works the bell loose and gets it in his mouth.

A wind-up musical mobile can be attractive, and of interest at all times, not just at baby's bedtime. Move it around, perhaps hanging it in front of your baby's bouncing chair or above the changing table. You can also make a "noisy" mobile by hanging rattles or bells from a coat hanger, or you can buy ones which make a clinking or chiming sound when the parts touch one another – pottery, metal or shells all make pleasing sounds. Hanging the mobile where it catches the breeze, or in a place where you can set it in motion as you go past, will help to maintain your baby's interest.

0 – 3 MONTHS

Touch and movement

At first, your baby may find the sensations of being lifted, carried and moved around rather overwhelming, especially if they are too sudden or he feels unsupported. He will prefer to be held closely and well wrapped. Some babies like to be swaddled when put down to sleep, to help provide the security they felt while in the womb. At first, many new babies may cry when being undressed, bathed or having their diaper changed. If your baby is very sensitive or irritable in this way, you will need to handle him calmly and quietly until he settles down. However, it won't be long before your baby begins to get used to life outside the womb and realizes that touch and the freedom to move his limbs can be exciting.

Bathtime fun
Bathtime provides the ideal opportunity to let your baby explore the world of touch and sensation. After the first few baths, which can be rather scary for both new parents and baby, most babies enjoy a wealth of sensations in their bath. They usually like the feel of the warm water around them and the freedom to move their limbs unencumbered by diapers and clothing. Many babies also enjoy being held skin to skin. If you have help around, try having a bath with your baby. Get into a warm (not hot) bath and take the baby on your lap or hold him against your chest. This is also a good way of helping a baby who does not like bathtime to enjoy being in the water.

Diaper-changing times also provide an opportunity for you to play with your baby. You can tickle him, blow raspberries on his tummy, count his toes and make bicycling movements with his legs. He may love the chance to move his arms and legs freely without his clothes or a diaper on, helping him to learn control of his body.

Textures
A young baby is aware of all sorts of different textures and

After the freedom of a bath, many babies enjoy being held close, wrapped snugly and securely in a warm towel.

needs to experience different kinds of sensations of touch. The feelings of lying without clothes on a sheepskin, a woolen rug, a soft blanket, a textured playmat or an activity rug can involve his whole body. Your baby may also like the texture of many soft toys; try stroking his face or tummy with their fur. You can also try putting safe objects with different textures into his hands once he has relaxed his newborn fist. Try things that are hard, soft, silky, coarse, furry, smooth. If the weather is warm enough, you can try taking off some of his clothes and laying him on different surfaces around the house, or let him feel a warm breeze on his skin in his carriage or on a rug in the garden.

Movement

Small babies like to be in motion, perhaps because it reminds them of their time in the womb. A walk in the carriage, being carried in a sling, being rocked in your arms will all soothe him and often send him to sleep. In the beginning he relies completely on you to provide this motion. As he grows, he realizes that he can

To help your baby learn that his touch and movement can achieve things, hold a rattle close enough for him to see and within easy reach of his hand. You can show him that the rattle makes a noise if he hits it and he can make it make a noise too.

make things move with his own body. A bouncing cradle gives him a new sensation of movement. You can rock it with your hand or foot to provide a soothing motion. Later, as he gets older, he will discover that by kicking his legs and waving his arms, he can make his bouncing cradle move too.

Using a sling or baby carrier has many advantages if your baby is wakeful or irritable. It frees your hands while your baby enjoys moving with you.

From about two months on, he will probably enjoy a chance to lie and kick his legs without a diaper on. Kicking can be made into a real game by hanging a balloon or soft ball within reach of his feet and letting him kick it, at first by chance but then with glee!

From two-and-a-half to three months, he may start to swipe at objects hung above his crib or carriage, or suspended in front of him when sitting on a lap or in his chair. This will enable him to realize that sometimes what he touches, moves.

By about three months he will be starting to grab hold of things, so remember to make sure they are safe for him if they do break loose.

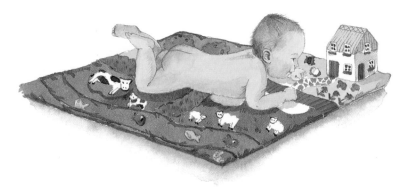

Your baby will enjoy the experience of feeling different textures. When he can hold his head up well, he can be placed on his front to look around.

Your child's progress

In three short months your baby progresses from a tiny, helpless being with strong inborn reflexes to grasp, make walking movements and to suck, to someone who can smile, coo, swipe and begin to grasp, lift up his head and make deliberate movements with his arms and legs. He experiences many different sensations and begins to sort out some routine from the many new things going on around him.

Looking and seeing
Your new baby can see from birth, focussing on objects held at 8–10in (20–25cm) from his face. He is usually most interested in human faces, but he also enjoys watching brightly-colored moving shapes, such as mobiles or a rattle held in your hand. Towards the end of his first twelve weeks he "finds" his hands and, for a time, watching them is his favorite amusement.

Hearing sounds
Your baby can hear and respond to sounds even while inside the womb. After birth he can be soothed by sounds which remind him of that time. By two to three months his gaze may be attracted by an object which makes a noise and he searches for it with his eyes. The sound of your voice will attract his attention and may soothe him.

Control of his hands
Your baby's hand is held in a tight fist from birth and grasps by reflex anything put into it. By about two months he can hold open his hand and by about three months he is able to choose to grasp something or not, though he won't be able to hold on to anything for long. By three months he begins to make random swipes at objects held within his reach.

Control of his body
At birth your newborn will lie with his head to one side, his knees bent up under his body and his bottom in the air. By about two months he has straightened out and can lift his head for a few moments, or lift it up when carried against your shoulder. By about three months he can lie on his tummy and push his head up by levering with his hands so he can look all around.

Social skills
Your baby smiles at about six weeks of age, though you may have noticed fleeting smiles earlier. He will usually smile at first only at the sight of a human face, and with the encouragement of smiles and voices. By three months he is likely to beam and may make cooing noises when you pick him up. He may also wriggle his whole body with delight.

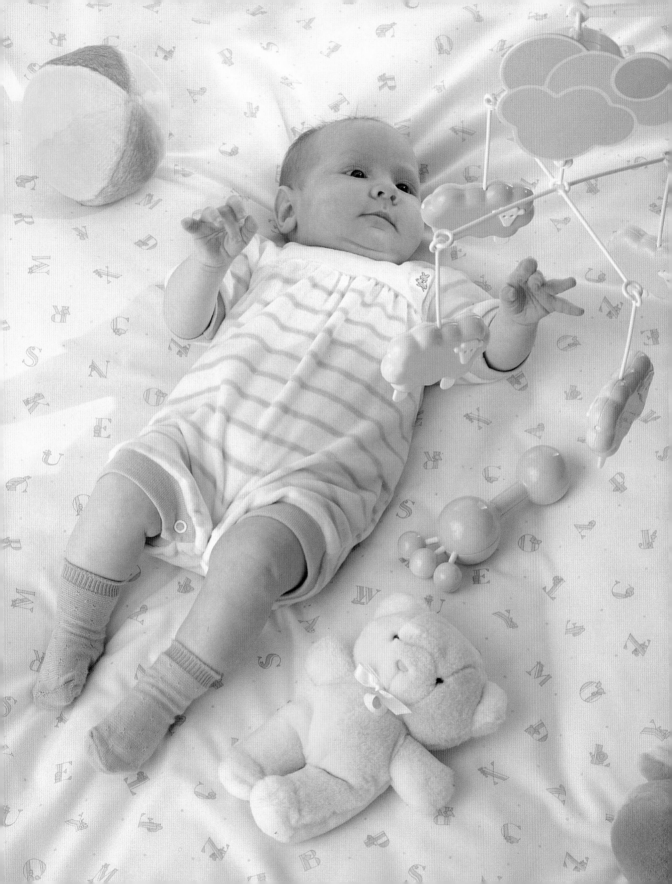

Starting to play

By the time she is three months old your baby becomes increasingly skilled at communicating her needs to you, with different cries to mean hunger, loneliness, tiredness or pain. She rewards you with more frequent smiles, gurgles and coos. She begins to grasp objects within her range, and reach out to touch things all around her. During this exciting time of enormous change, she is intensely curious and wants to touch, hold, put into her mouth, feel and explore everything around her. You need to provide a steady flow of fresh things to play with that will interest and stimulate her, from rattles and soft toys to household objects that she can handle safely to encourage better control of her hands. As her ability to use her hands improves she benefits from toys that move or make a noise when she touches them, or that she can take apart and examine. It is also vital to talk and sing to her and give her a chance to respond, as looking, listening and starting to make a wide variety of sounds are essential for her to develop her language skills. She also needs a wide variety of experiences outside the home – trips to the park and shops and new, friendly faces.

Things to grab and hold

fact, her hands may be the first things she puts in her mouth. After that, anything will go into her mouth. This is a natural way for her to investigate objects, and using her mouth in this way is as important as using her hands. This means that you have to be very careful that she can't get hold of things that could hurt her – anything dirty, sharp, pointed or small enough to be swallowed must be kept out of her reach. While her mouth is so sensitive, and particularly when she is teething, she will want to chew on things. Make sure that she has teething rings, objects made of thick plastic, rubber or smooth wood, or material such as a dish towel when she wants to chew.

Rattles
Rattles are very satisfying toys and your baby will continue to enjoy them as she learns to explore the different possibilities that some of them offer. They come in all sorts of different shapes, sizes, textures and colors, and make a variety of sounds. Some have moving parts on the inside or outside, and some have suction pads to stick them to a smooth surface. Some are in the form of a key-ring, and others are concealed inside soft toys. Try to choose rattles that have a small enough part to fit comfortably in your baby's hand. A good selection of rattles will give your child lasting pleasure if you look out for those that will adapt as your baby's play develops.

Once a baby can reach out and grab something, she will love to explore a variety of new objects that she can hold in her hand and put in her mouth.

As your baby becomes stronger and her focus improves, she will start using her eyes and hands together, reaching out for things, taking hold of them deliberately and bringing them up to inspect them with her eyes and mouth. She wants to put everything in her mouth at this stage because this helps her to understand more about the shape and feel of things. She uses her mouth to explore in preference to her hands. In

18

A key-ring rattle, for example, may be used as car-keys by a toddler while a clown with a rattle inside may become a favorite cuddly toy.

Exploring through feeling
As your baby's grip becomes stronger she will be able to hold a wider variety of things and experience the difference between things that are large and small, light and heavy, soft and hard. Some things that you will have around the house can be useful at this stage because her curiosity is endless and things that you take for granted will be new and different for her. All objects are playthings for your baby.

She may become more aware of different textures and would enjoy a "feely board" you can make yourself by securely gluing things of different textures (corduroy, velvet, shiny card, textured

At about five or six months, she holds objects in her palm, using her hand like a scoop. By the age of about nine months she uses her fingers more, rather than her whole hand. By the time she is about twelve months old, she will have developed quite fine skills in picking up objects with a "pincer" grip, using her thumb and forefinger in an accurate and deliberate way. She can also poke and point with her index finger, coordinating her hands and eyes.

hardboard) to a cardboard surface. Because so many toys are made of smooth, hard plastic, it's important for her to find out about other textures too, such as wood, metal, sponge and cloth.

Other toys that she can handle and explore at this age are plastic safety mirrors that she can glimpse herself in, solidly made little cars with wheels that she can spin and soft toys that squeak when she squeezes them.

Playing with your baby
Although your baby will play on her own for short periods, she needs you to be around to cuddle her, carry her, talk to her, to pick up things she's dropped or which have rolled out of reach, to put objects back into her hand and to check that she is not going to hurt herself with anything. As you play with her, it is important to let her try to do things for herself. If you hold something within her reach, let her use her eyes and hands to find it, giving her time to work out what she has to do. This may take patience on your part, but will be much more rewarding for you both when she succeeds.

Remember that at this stage your baby will be better off playing at any one time with a few selected objects rather than being swamped with a heap of toys. She can't concentrate on more than one thing at a time, and too many toys will distract her from the all-important task of exploring something fully.

Household articles may interest your baby as much as her own toys. She will enjoy banging a saucepan with a wooden spoon or rattling a small can that she can't open, filled with dried beans.

Purposeful play

From about six months your baby will be learning to sit, supported at first, then on her own. She may be able to roll over from her back now and may even be making her first attempts at crawling. She'll be wanting toys which do something whether they squeak, have moving parts or bits that disappear when pushed. Toys that she can do things with will help to develop her skills in picking up, holding and using objects as well as helping her to understand more about the physical properties objects possess.

Using hands together

By six months, your baby may be starting to pass objects from one hand to the other but if you hand her another toy, she will drop what she is already holding to reach out for the new one because she can still concentrate on only one thing at a time. By seven or eight months she will be trying to see what things can do; she will bang them on the floor or table to see if they make a noise or may wave or shake them to see what happens. She may now hold on to two different objects at the same time for a short while, but is unlikely to bang them together yet.

As her manipulative skills develop she learns that she can use her hands and arms together – to bang toys together, to lift a large object, even to pull things apart. She'll use her arms to reach up to you when she wants to be picked up or cuddled. However, she can't let go of things of her own accord. Once she has grabbed an earring or got hold of a lock of hair it can be very hard to persuade her to release it.

Letting go

Soon she will begin to play with a purpose, wanting to see the effect of her actions. She will gradually learn to let go of things when she wants, and you can make quite a game of this with her. She will start

Letting go is a hand skill that has to be learned. Once it is, though, it becomes an activity that delights many children.

dropping or throwing things out of her crib, carriage or highchair and will enjoy this even more if you protest pleasantly but loudly as you put them back. You can give her different things to drop from her highchair and if you place a metal tray where they fall she will see and hear that a ball will hit with a clang, then bounce and roll away, a bean-bag will plop and a plastic or metal object will clatter or clang.

Another game you can play is to pass her an object, then hold out your hand and ask for it back. This will delight her and keep you both busy for ages!

Making things happen

With her new-found hand control, she will enjoy toys that "do" something. If you spend some time showing her how an activity center works with its different knobs, handles, dials and revolving balls and drums, she will soon learn to operate some of its moving parts herself. Some make a variety of satisfying sounds as well as having moving parts and these provide additional interest and stimulation. Your baby may continue to enjoy an activity center after her first birthday, operating the different parts with more and more skill.

A telephone is another very popular toy. At first she enjoys just removing and replacing the receiver and pulling the phone around by the receiver cord. Then she will discover the fun of pushing the buttons or dialling. Since dialling is harder to achieve, she will find it a more interesting challenge. When choosing a toy

At this age, a toy telephone encourages pointing, poking and two-handed play.

telephone look for a robust one that makes satisfying noises. Cheap toy telephones are unlikely to stand up to the wear and tear they get – a good toy telephone will be played with for several years, becoming a prop in "let's pretend" games and encouraging language development.

Surprise toys and games

Just as they enjoy hide and seek, babies of this age often enjoy toys which pop up and surprise them. A good toy for a baby to use on her own is a pop-up toy where long peg

men bounce up on springs when she presses them lightly with her index finger. She may also quickly learn to remove the men and fit them back in the holes. A pop-up clown in a cone which you show her will also delight her, especially if you hold the cone so that she can push the stick up to make the clown appear herself. Many babies love a jack-in-the-box, though some may be alarmed by the ones that make a very loud noise. If your child is frightened, put the toy away for a few weeks and try it again when she is a little older. Or, to start with, choose a toy that doesn't make a noise.

You can also play a game with her that shows her the effects of her actions. When she is between nine months and one year old, wait until she makes a definite action – like banging a toy – and say "boo!" When she does it again, say "boo" again. Soon she will be banging deliberately to make you say "boo" and you'll both laugh when you do.

Toys that a child can operate herself and see the results demonstrate cause and effect.

Beginning to explore

As her first birthday approaches, your baby will begin to combine her newly acquired abilities to sit up on her own and perhaps to move – be it by crawling, walking or shuffling on her bottom – with the natural curiosity that babies and children possess. She'll be into everything and she may still be putting things in her mouth to explore them. By trying to see her surroundings from her point of view, you can remove anything from her reach that is potentially dangerous or that you don't want her to get hold of.

Emptying . . .
One of her favorite pastimes will be emptying things out of whatever container she can get hold of and then examining the emptied out items. She will enjoy taking things out of drawers and cupboards, waste baskets and her toybox and tipping things out of packets. She often will inspect every item carefully, though sometimes she may simply enjoy seeing everything spill out in a heap.

Emptying a cupboard will be absolutely absorbing. She will look at everything in it, clapping things together or banging them on the floor, before discarding them and moving on to the next thing she can find.

At this stage you could set aside for her a drawer or cupboard in the kitchen with items she can safely empty and explore. She will also love going through your handbag or any bag or box left within her reach. You can give her an old handbag, a small suitcase with a lid that won't trap her fingers or a cardboard box with a lid, filled with a selection of items such as spare keys on a ring, a small purse, an old train

Water is endlessly fascinating to explore. It can't be held, makes you wet, has no definite shape and suddenly spills when you least expect it! When your baby is playing in or with water, you should always stay with her to supervise as well as to share in the enjoyment.

All sorts of items in a bag or box intrigue a child as she empties them out and investigates each one closely.

timetable or diary, an old powder compact, some paper, picture postcards or greeting cards with bright pictures, a ball of wool, a small hairbrush, a small safety mirror. You can also add one or two favorite toys. Keep her interested and satisfy her curiosity by varying what's in it from time to time.

... and filling
When she is nearly a year old your baby may discover that she can also put objects into a container as well as taking them out. At first, she may simply be delighted to realize that she can put a brick inside a plastic cup; she will put it in, tip it out, then put it back in over and over again, fascinated by the fact that the object disappears and reappears every time. She will try out different objects and discover that some are too big to fit; as she plays she will be working out many important ideas about the nature of objects, how they behave and their relative shapes and sizes.

Pouring play
Water makes emptying and filling games even more fun. Whether your baby is playing in the bath or with a dish-washing bowl or baby bath on the floor, you can help her to fill up plastic cups or other safe containers with water and empty them out again. Give her plastic jugs and toy teapots with spouts which pour easily, stacking cups with different-sized holes in the bottom, from which the water will sprinkle or pour out, a small sieve and "play buckets" with holes in different places. These will encourage her to fill them herself for the fun of seeing the water gush or trickle out.

Handling shapes
Although most babies under one are only just beginning to develop the skills to use them, now is the time to think about introducing a simple shape sorter and set of stacking cups. With shape sorters, round shapes are the easiest for your child, then square ones, then more complex shapes like triangles.

At first she may simply enjoy emptying the shapes out of the container without its lid on and rolling the stacking cups around on the floor or clapping them together. If you show her how the shapes fit or how the cups nest inside each other, it won't be long before she starts to enjoy pushing them down and watching them disappear or trying to fit the cups together. However, if she shows little interest, put the toys away and let her try them again some time later.

At this age you can also introduce some very simple construction toys such as bristle blocks, which she can easily fit together and pull apart. However, initially, she may have the most fun emptying the box and perhaps putting some of the blocks back into it again.

Stacking cups and a simple shape sorter provide your child with lots of fun at this age and for a long time to come.

23

Toys for sitters and movers

Once she can hold her head up, your baby may enjoy lying on her tummy. As her back and shoulders get stronger, her hands are free to play with and manipulate the toys on the floor around her. Or, she may prefer to be propped up in a sitting position, surrounded by her toys. However, in this position she may need her hands for balance so she is not free to use them to explore. Gradually balance and strength develop so that she can sit up independently.

Sitting and playing

If your baby is a "sitter," toys that aren't going to roll away too readily, and that are interesting for her to handle and explore, are essential. She will enjoy rattles on suction pads which can be fixed to a

Toys on rounded bases or those that won't roll away are good for a sitting child.

smooth floor, highchair tray or even the wall or door; pull-along toys which you can teach her to pull towards her if they stray too far and any toys to bang, shake and feel.

Another very good toy for this stage is a set of colorful stacking rings on a pole. These will get lots of use – to chew on, to throw and to poke her hands and fingers through – long before she gets the idea of trying to stack them, let alone learning to stack them in anything like the right order.

Your baby cannot be expected to sit and play for long – she will get bored unless you give her a change of scene and different toys to play with. Try keeping some of her toys back rather than letting her have them all every day. Then you have something new to offer when she seems bored. You can also try changing her position, putting her on her front for a different view of her surroundings.

The stage when your child can sit up unsupported with toys which she can explore may be one of the easiest and most delightful. Or, it may be a time when she becomes frustrated at not being able to reach or get things that have rolled away and so needs a lot more attention and active entertaining.

Although she may be "sitting," you will soon find that your baby has moved from where you left her, by shuffling on her bottom or making slow progress as she reaches out for an object that may have moved out of her range. Still, a placid child can be quite content to sit in one place and although she has the ability to move – either by shuffling on her bottom or by rolling, if not by crawling or walking – she doesn't have much inclination to do so, especially if all her toys are within easy reach. You can encourage her to become

Exciting toys that move easily delight a mobile child. Any toys that roll along or can be pushed are enjoyed – especially if they make a jolly sound too.

more adventurous in several ways. You can try leaving a cupboard that is full of safe and exciting objects temptingly open where she can see it, or move a favorite toy just out of her range. Blowing bubbles which are within her reach for a time but then move off or rolling a clangy toy or ball towards her but just out of reach may make her move too, without even realizing she's done so.

However, she will only move in a purposeful way when she has the physical ability to do so. To try to force her to move before she's ready will be frustrating for both of you. If

she is upset by not being able to reach something, although she has tried, then it is best to move it within her reach. She will soon be on the go, when she's ready.

She's off!
Some time around six months your baby is likely to be supporting herself on her hands and knees with her legs brought forward under her body, rocking backwards and forwards. When she is about eight months she may be able to make some progress by kicking with her legs and pressing her hands back against the floor. Because she

has more control and strength in her arms, her first attempts to crawl can push her backwards, and these movements may well frustrate her if they take her further from where she is trying to go.

Once your baby can crawl efficiently, and this can happen almost overnight, she will love chasing after toys which roll and move. She'll be fascinated by push'n'go toys, though at first you may have to press the button that sets them in motion for her.

Crawling can be very uncomfortable on a rough carpet or floor if her knees are exposed. Light trousers, even in summer, help to protect her.

Movement games

When she is very young, your baby will depend on you to provide the framework and encouragement for her to develop her muscular strength and control. With you holding her securely, she'll enjoy the experience of standing and "feeling her feet."

Throughout these months your baby is gradually getting stronger and gaining more control over her whole body. You can help her to develop the physical skills she will use in learning to crawl and walk. With lots of physical exercise she develops both muscular strength and control of her arms and legs.

Games to play
Babies love to roll, bounce, kick, reach and "dance."

Before she can do any of these things alone, your baby will enjoy games that help her to experience these movements. At around three or four months she will enjoy being held on your knee and gently bounced so that she feels her feet while you support her weight. Some babies at around five or six months enjoy short spells in a baby bouncer suspended from a doorway, but don't put her in one until she can support her head for long periods.

Your three- or four-month-old baby will still enjoy being laid on a mat, preferably with her diaper off, for a good kick. She may start to roll over, first from her side to her back, then from her back to her side and over to her tummy. You will find there are all sorts of physical games you can play with your baby to your mutual delight. Her enthusiasm and enjoyment are immensely satisfying. Sitting on your knee and being bounced in rhythm to a nursery rhyme, being lifted up into the air, wiggled around and returned to a safe place on your lap, being helped to sit up from lying down to the tune of "Row, row, row your boat" are fun for you both, bringing you into close contact. If your baby is bored or fretful, try turning on some music, picking her up and taking her as your partner for a dance around the room.

Splash!
Your baby will love the freedom of kicking, splashing and wriggling in the bath now. Until she can sit securely you

will need to hold her, and when she starts to move about more you will need to have a hand ready to catch her if she slips. But with your steadying hand she should feel safe to splash and you can encourage her to "swim."

Once she has had her first two sets of immunizations, you can take her swimming if there is a suitable pool near you. She may well be happy to splash and "swim" in your arms although she may fret if the pool is very noisy or if she gets unexpectedly splashed.

Musical toys and games
As your baby gets older, she will increasingly join in with songs and musical games. At first she may just chuckle and laugh, but soon she will start to anticipate what's coming next and may hold her breath and wriggle as she does. She may learn to clap her hands or make

A drum to bang or maracas to shake are lots of fun and make instant noise that stops when the action stops.

other actions which fit in with the song. You may still find it helpful to follow a book or tape of nursery rhymes to broaden your repertoire.

A musical box which plays a tune when you or she open it, press a button or pull a string will encourage her to listen and wait for the tune to end so that she can make it start again.

"Finger games" like "This little piggy went to market"

will help your baby learn to anticipate what will happen. Try exaggerating the actions and the final pause before the tickle to give her plenty of time to respond. Toys can add variety to these games. You can introduce a soft toy or doll to do the tickling, or use a squeaky toy to surprise her. The game may send her into fits of giggles and she'll make it clear she wants you to tickle her again and again.

Exercises
You can try some simple exercises which you and your baby can play together, and which can benefit both of you. Try the following:

Flying:
Lie on your back with your knees raised. Lift your baby up so that she is resting on your shins which you lift off the floor. Hold her arms to support her and so that she's looking at your face. Raise your knees; lift her arms into the air.

Push-ups:
When your baby can hold her head up well, put her on her tummy, with her arms out in front of her. Hold her hips and lift her up into the "wheelbarrow" position. Lower her; repeat.

First words

Your baby already has a
number of ways of
communicating what she
wants, although she may not
actually say a single word as
such until she is at least nine
months old and probably
nearer a year. She is learning
about communication
throughout her early months
and needs to listen to the
sound of your voice, and to
"talk" back at you. She may
keep up a constant flow of
noise from the middle of her
first year, trying out different
sounds, blowing bubbles and
raspberries, using her mouth in
all sorts of ways.

Your child understands
words long before she can talk
herself; she will probably
respond to her name by
turning and looking when her
name is called when she is
eight or nine months old.

As well as understanding a
lot of what you say to her, she
will also understand the tone of
your voice. She'll know when
you're cross even before she
understands "no," and she'll
know when you're pleased as
well. Remember to talk to her
constantly, pointing out things
to her and telling her what you
are doing. Even if you think
much of it is over her head, her
understanding is growing more
and more.

First books
Your baby can start to enjoy
books with you from very early
on. You can look at them with
her, talking about what each
picture shows. Soon she will
begin to recognize the pictures
and link them to the object
they represent. More than
anything she will enjoy the
closeness of sitting with you

Your baby's early babble is an
essential stage in her learning to
talk, and is encouraged by you
"conversing" with her. Speak in
simple words, clearly and
naturally, to help her understand
and learn. Don't feel self-
conscious about doing this; she is
loving the attention and learning a
great deal about communicating.

Early books need to be robust and easy to clean. When they're not being read they may well be sucked and chewed!

and listening to you talk. Left to explore books on her own, she will find them to be interesting objects to pick up, open, shut and chew. Board books are good at first and come in various forms. They can open in different ways too – like a fan or an accordion.

Rag books can also be useful; they are good for chewing as well as looking at and are virtually indestructible. You can also let your child loose on glossy magazines or thick catalogues you've finished with. She'll enjoy trying to turn the pages, looking at the pictures and also screwing up the paper. Many babies are in fact fascinated by paper and will spend hours scrunching it, tearing it and throwing it. Try to discourage her from chewing it though.

Hide and seek games
A favorite game in these months is the traditional "Peek-a-boo," which will delight your baby from the age of three months. At first, sit close to her and cover your face with your hands, then open them and say

"boo!" Then try slowly peeping round the edge of your fingers or moving your hands up and down to expose your face. You can hide behind a chair or door and pop out, or just turn your head away and back again. As your baby gets older, she may try hiding her own face. You can also try putting a diaper or cloth over her head which you or she can pull away, although this alarms some babies at first. "Peek-a-boo" delights your baby so much because at first she is unaware that an object is permanent – if she drops it, it is as if it has disappeared from the face of the earth. She is not sure that you haven't disappeared too – which is why it's such a relief to her to see you reappear again.

As your baby gets older she starts to understand that things still exist when she can't see them. This is the age to start some simple "hide and seek" games. At first, "hide" an object under a see-through plastic container or sieve and see if she can "find" it. Then try covering a toy with a cloth or towel – again while she is looking – and see if she lifts the towel to "discover" it. You can

help by peeping if she doesn't get the idea at first or letting a part of the toy "stick out." You can also try hiding things under stacking cups or other containers – do this while your baby is looking so that she knows what to do.

You can start to play "talking" games with your baby too. Sit together facing one another or next to each other in front of a mirror and point out things to her – Daddy's nose, Sarah's nose, Daddy's eyes, Sarah's eyes and so on. She'll enjoy the game even though she may be too young to say anything or point to a feature or part of her body herself.

With games like these, and in all your talking with your baby, be natural and not too repetitive. Remember you are talking to a real person, who will soon be able to understand and respond.

By about nine months your baby may copy simple actions like clapping and waving. Following later may be an attempt to copy your words as well, that becomes a clear and ringing "bye-bye."

Your child's progress

Your baby's development in the first year is astonishingly rapid. She learns to use her hands to grasp and hold and to use objects in a more complex way. She also uses her mouth to explore objects fully. She gains more control of her body, learning to hold her head up, sit upright, crawl and stand. She develops her social skills, learning to laugh, babble and to use a word or two. She forms increasingly strong ties with her parents and other carers.

Looking and touching

During her first twelve months your baby becomes able to see both close up and at a distance. She can follow a moving object by moving her head as well as her eyes. She can copy you if you show her how simple toys work and press buttons or levers to operate them. She loves looking at books, recognizing a large number of objects in the pictures.

Learning to hold

By her first birthday your baby can reach out and pick up objects and examine them with one or both hands, and she can push, let go or throw them away too. She uses a pincer grip to pick up small objects between her thumb and forefinger and uses her index finger to poke and point. She can also put some objects inside or on top of others.

Sitting, crawling and standing

By seven or eight months your baby may be sitting unsupported. By ten months she may start pulling herself upright on furniture and learns to walk around it using her hands for support. By eight or nine months of age your baby may crawl well, or she may miss out on crawling especially if she prefers to stand and walk.

Social skills

By her first birthday your baby may be attached to her mother or main care giver and may show great distress if left. She needs a lot of one-to-one attention and may react with fear to strangers. She is most secure if she has a daily routine and may be distressed by change. By eleven months she may adopt something as a comfort object (see page 39).

Learning to communicate

At one year your baby may babble constantly, at times sounding as if she is using a language all her own. She has "conversations" with you and understands a few words and may even use one or two. She may understand "no" and simple commands like "give me" or "look." She may point at things she wants and recognize familiar objects in pictures in a book.

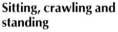

On the go

In the coming year your child will change dramatically, becoming more mobile and developing greater understanding and communication skills. Not only is he starting to talk, he can also express himself in a variety of ways such as shouting, babbling, pointing, laughing and crying. He learns to walk, run, climb and jump, and with his increased mobility can reach and explore things that were formerly beyond his grasp, at times seeming to have elastic arms. His curiosity is unbounded and he needs careful handling to ensure that he has plenty of opportunities to learn and explore and through a wide variety of experiences to extend all his senses and still remain safe. As his control of his hands improves, he needs toys to build, stack, fill, fit together and sort. He needs, too, larger scale toys that test his physical abilities and increase his confidence: things to push, pull, ride and scoot on. At the same time, he begins to become aware of himself as a person. He learns a great deal by copying and imitating the things that you and others in the family do, becoming aware of the routines in his daily life. He needs a wide variety of experiences – going for a bus or train ride and visits to family and friends are all important for him.

Outdoor play

When she is ready, encourage your child to climb up the ladder of a slide. This helps her to coordinate the movements of her hands, arms and legs.

As your baby grows into a toddler, steadier on his feet and more active, he needs the opportunity to play outdoors to master the skills of walking, running, climbing and jumping. If your child is very active and your garden is large enough, you may want to set up a small slide or jungle gym at some time after his first birthday.

An older baby or young child will also enjoy a garden swing as long as he is secure and can't fall out.

A trip to a park or playground – especially if it has an area for under-fives – will present your child with many new challenges and experiences. Your older baby will enjoy swings and see-saws if you hold him on, and also likes being slid down a small slide. Take care that you don't push him too far for his sense of safety and give him a fright that will put him off in the future. Try to maintain a balance so that his adventurous spirit is encouraged while taking care to protect him from real danger. Children of this age are robust and are often very sensible about knowing what they can and can't attempt, so let him do as much as he can by himself, with you standing by just in case he tumbles.

Balance and coordination
Your child will love just playing with you in an open space which gives him the chance to toddle and eventually to run about freely. He will enjoy playing with a ball with you to show him how to roll it, run after it and push it along.

Fun with water and sand
Apart from sheer physical exercise, outdoor play gives scope for other activities too. Playing with water is more

satisfying out of doors as well as being easier to organize. One good game is to give your child a large brush and a tub of water and let him "paint" an outside wall or fence or paving stones. This is particularly convincing if the surface changes color when wet, as many do. Or, you can unroll a spare roll of wallpaper for him to paint on.

A paddling pool, lawn sprinkler, watering cans and a hose are excellent and endless fun on hot days in the summer. Bubbles are fun anytime. A few drops of dishwashing liquid in a bowl of water will produce lots of bubbles if you blow into it with a straw or your child can make bubbles just by splashing! You can buy plastic containers of bubble mixture, or make your own using one part of dishwashing liquid to two parts water. Your child will love watching the bubbles and chasing them in the breeze. However, it will be a while before he can blow them.

At this age, your child is ready to play with sand. Make clear rules that sand is never to be thrown or eaten. An old

At this age and for a long time to come, sand provides an excellent play medium.

plastic tub filled with washed sand will give your child plenty of opportunity to experiment. Let him feel the difference between dry sand, which pours rather like water, and wet sand which goes solid and can be used to mold into shapes. If he pours water on to dry sand himself he'll see the change that takes place.

Noting nature
Your toddler may be intrigued by creatures he finds living in the garden or park. Go hunting under flower-pots and stones for snails, and put them on a smooth warm surface like the top of a wall or a paving stone

A lifelong love of nature can start with trips to the park to feed the ducks. Point out small details to your child and he soon learns to be very observant and comes to appreciate all forms of life.

and watch the snail come out of its shell and move. Your child may also be fascinated by beetles, spiders, worms and other insects, especially if you can overcome any fear or prejudices you may have. He may love watching birds, too, feeding at a bird table or from nuts or suet hung on the branch of a tree.

The sense of smell
While you're out together in the garden, you can help your child to begin to notice that some flowers, herbs, newly-cut grass, pine needles and wet earth all have different smells. He will soon learn how to use his sense of smell if you stop to sniff the flowers when you're out on a walk or in the garden and pause to breathe in the smells as you go into the bakery or fish store.

Toys to push and ride

When your child "finds his feet" he will, at first, pull himself up to a standing position and then be stuck there until you gently lower him again. Soon, once he is firmly confident on his feet, he will start to "cruise" around the furniture, holding on to anything that is the right height. Then he will take his first exciting independent steps, but holding on when he can until he feels really steady. Pushalong toys and later, when he can walk well, toys he can ride, will be tremendous fun for him and improve his balance and confidence. And, whether he is pushing or riding, he will need to plan where he is going and to work out what to do when he gets stuck in a tight place.

Toys to push
A sturdy pushalong toy, such as a pushcart, is very useful when your baby reaches the cruising stage. The cart you choose should be stable enough so that it won't tip over as he puts his weight on the handles to pull himself up, and heavy enough so that it won't run away with him as he pushes it along, practicing his walking skills. If you find that it tips easily or moves too quickly for him, you can add extra weight to it until he is steadier on his feet. He can also load his toys into the cart and take them out again.

As his walking progresses so that he can walk confidently on his own, other pushalong toys will be suitable. Your child may enjoy a toy stroller now, since they are usually too light for a child who is not walking well. Once he is walking confidently he will find a stroller great fun to push along. Like full-sized strollers, they come in a variety of models. As your child grows, the stroller becomes a great make-believe toy as teddies and dolls can be taken out in it.

Pushalong toys which make a noise are very popular, too. Again they come in many varieties: chiming ones – usually a revolving cylinder that makes a melodic sound or has balls inside to rattle – or those which hum or click. Other pushalongs are shaped like an

A ride-on toy adds a new dimension to your child's mobility. She soon learns to push herself along, sometimes at quite a speed and with great excitement. These toys also help her to gain confidence and improve her balance.

animal with whirring legs or a lawnmower which makes an appropriate racket and has the added appeal of enabling him to copy what he sees you doing. They should be robust enough to stay on the ground without pressure.

Ride-on toys

Some pushalong toys can also be ridden and these, whether in the shape of a vehicle or an animal, are very popular and extremely versatile. You can get durable plastic cars which may have a removable handle attached to the back, others have a handle permanently fixed on, others have no handle at all. These often have features that your child may grow into such as a horn on the steering wheel or a seat that lifts up to reveal a "trunk."

Some toddler trikes without pedals also have a handle at the back for pushing along. Trikes are narrower than the cars, so your child will be able to reach the floor more easily. Since such a wide selection of ride-on toys is available, it is important to choose carefully to find ones that are sturdy enough not to tip over and a height that the child can climb on and off safely himself.

Large stuffed animals on wheels are also very popular both to push and to ride. Again these should be stable and a size your child can climb onto.

A rocking toy, whether shaped like a boat or an animal, is great fun. At first, you may have to hold a young toddler on and rock him gently. As he grows he'll be able to climb on and rock himself.

His first hesitant attempts at walking involve sliding his feet and hands along, progressing to holding on with one hand until he can grasp something to support him with his other hand, then lurching from one support to the next. He'll one day find himself standing without support – and immediately drop to his bottom! However, he'll quickly regain his confidence and try again. (*right*)

Soon he will be able to combine a few unsteady, unsupported steps with holding on. He will walk with his arms held high for balance, and hold on when he can. (*left*)

Within a few months he will be walking more steadily and confidently, with his arms by his side. He can also stand up from sitting on his own. (*right*)

Children of this age enjoy pushing along almost anything. Even a cardboard box can become a car to push a teddy in.

Copying and imitating

As your child develops from a baby into a toddler, he will become much more aware of what you do and say. He will want to be with you and to do what you do. He will love to be allowed to "help" you with the dishes, loading the washing-machine, making the beds, emptying shopping bags – whatever you are doing. He will want to be where you are, and if he's not "helping" you, he will want to be imitating what he has seen you do. While you're busy in the kitchen, give him a few plastic plates, yogurt pots and spoons in a plastic tub with warm water placed at a safe height. Though his clothes and the

Your child can set up tea parties for his dolls, teddies, brothers and sisters – and you.

floor may well get soaked, his enjoyment is immense because he can do something that he has seen you doing.

Imitative toys
A toy tea-set provides your child with plenty of play opportunities and is invaluable for encouraging speech and language skills. It is an ideal toy to link real life with copying and imitating games.

A child's play is very much in the here and now. She may tenderly tuck a teddy into a crib one minute, only to whip it out by one leg the next when she decides to put her doll in the crib instead!

A toy telephone remains popular at this stage, though the way your child uses it changes. He may now pick it up and hold the receiver to his ear in imitation of you. Later he may begin to have "conversations" – babbling with the occasional word that you can understand – interspersed.

Simple cloth play houses are available or you can make one yourself out of chairs with blankets draped over. A cardboard box, a small child's chair or upturned waste basket to sit on and a table – perhaps made from a plastic storage box or cardboard carton – can be added to furnish the house.

Pull-along toys

Other simple toys such as those that are pulled along can help your young toddler develop imaginative play. They also encourage coordination and balance as the child looks behind him as he walks along. He will have to be steady on his feet to master a pull-along, but will love taking a toy dog for a walk. Look for pull-alongs which are very stable – if they keep falling over they will only frustrate him. A toy with moving parts bobbing up and down as it moves along, or one that makes a satisfying noise, is even more fascinating and the noise will help you to keep track of him as he walks off.

Dolls and soft toys

Dolls and soft toys take on different roles and provide an outlet for your child's feelings in his pretend play. You can make the toy "come to life", making it talk, and walk, and

A play house is fascinating as a place to make into a pretend home of a child's own.

your child will soon be copying you. Even if he is still at the one-word stage, he may soon talk to a teddy or doll and what he says and his tone of voice will probably sound very familiar to you!

Look for dolls that are robust, have eyes that open and shut, since babies and toddlers find these fascinating, and can be undressed. He will also enjoy immensely a doll that he can bathe. They need to

be large enough to provide a satisfying but comfortable armful; the right size for a toy stroller or crib is ideal.

Teddies, other furry animals and cloth toys like clowns and rag dolls are also popular. They are often cuddly and particularly nice to hold.

Comfort objects

For all his imitating of you and trying to be grown up, your child is still very young and needs plenty of comfort and reassurance. Some children become attached to a particular toy or blanket. It can become a prized possession that must go with him wherever he goes.

It may be seen as an extra link to you until you are there to comfort him when he is tired, ill or upset, especially if you always tuck him in with it at bedtime or give it to him when he's fretful.

It may be a good idea to have an identical one to give him when the other is being washed, if he allows you to take it away, or if it is lost or damaged. He may notice the difference and see it as second best but in the end will realize that it's still better than nothing or he may get attached to something else instead.

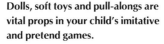

Dolls, soft toys and pull-alongs are vital props in your child's imitative and pretend games.

Stacking and fitting

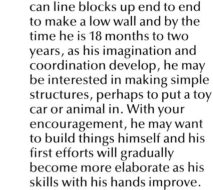

can line blocks up end to end to make a low wall and by the time he is 18 months to two years, as his imagination and coordination develop, he may be interested in making simple structures, perhaps to put a toy car or animal in. With your encouragement, he may want to build things himself and his first efforts will gradually become more elaborate as his skills with his hands improve.

Blocks for an older baby or young toddler need to be large, easy to hold and fit together and include basic, square blocks as well as several different shapes. Bristle blocks are fun at this age too. They are easy for little fingers to put

together and take apart and can make interesting and colorful shapes of infinite variety.

Stacking
A toddler who enjoys putting blocks together may like stacking all sorts of different objects. He can experience

Empty cereal boxes, empty spools, plastic tubs – lots of things – are all fun to stack.

Playing with blocks is one way that a child begins to put objects together. At about 12 months he may stack two or three blocks on top of one another and then knock them down.

For several months before his first birthday your child was studying objects closely. By using his hands and eyes together he is beginning to understand more about objects, seeing their different shapes and sizes and how they relate to each other. He is also gaining better control over his finger movements, making him more dextrous and better able to handle objects. His increasing ability to use his hands improves with practice and leads to the skills needed later for drawing and writing.

He will enjoy watching you build things with his blocks, especially if you build a tall tower for him to demolish. He

how different shapes and sizes fit together; how larger objects work best at the bottom, with smaller ones on top.

Many stacking toys are also available and these have the advantage of being precisely

guide his finger in the beginning.

You can also get toys made up of a series of different colored balls which thread on poles of different heights. Or you can collect an assortment of plastic containers like yogurt

Toys that stack or nest encourage a child to use both hands and coordinate his hand movements with his eyes. He also starts to be aware of differences in size and shape, large and small.

graduated so they stack and fit together easily. Different colored stacking cups are an excellent toy especially if they have a rim which holds them together when they are stacked. He will see that these must be stacked in a certain order – the largest at the bottom – if all the cups are to be used. You can start him off with the three or four largest cups while he gets used to the idea of stacking them in order.

Other stacking toys are based on a central pole with rings or discs with holes in the middle to fit on it.

Figures which stack on top of one another and pop into the air when a button is pressed are especially fun and add an element of surprise. He'll love seeing the "cause and effect" of pressing the button to make the toy jump up. However, the button can be quite stiff and you may need to

cups for your child to stack and fit together.

Fitting together
As well as being interested in stacking your child starts to find all kinds of toys and objects that fit together interesting too. This is the age at which toddlers become fascinated with putting pegs in holes, keys in locks and nesting things inside one another; they also like opening and shutting boxes of all kinds. Young toddlers also like taking lids on and off, to see if there's anything inside. Different-sized saucepans are favorites as are plastic containers and large plastic bottles and jars with screw tops.

The "hide and seek" idea is still popular at this age and the element of surprise – will there be another, smaller object inside? – makes nesting toys fascinating. Your child will like fitting together traditional Russian dolls and putting a graded set of stacking cups inside one another.

The skill he uses to unscrew lids and take nesting toys apart involves his wrists as well as his hands. These movements enable him to turn on taps and open doors as well as play with the knobs on a hi-fi or television. Shapes which thread like a nut onto a screw build on this skill as long as the shapes and the screw are large enough for him to manage comfortably.

Making connections

As he plays, your child is processing information from his eyes and his hands. He is not doing something in isolation or just thinking in an abstract way. From his close study of objects and his experiences of handling and stacking them, he observes that they have properties that are similar and different. He begins to understand that things fall into various categories: different sizes, shapes, colors and functions.

Blocks and simple stacking toys can be used to extend this awareness. You can describe them by their color and shape names to help your child get accustomed to these different concepts. If you use precise descriptive words such as

Your child loves sorting out the apples from the oranges in the fruit bowl or the dark clothes from the whites in the laundry basket, especially if he's doing it to "help."

Sorting objects gives your child experience in handling things with different shapes and textures, looking out for what is the same about them and what is different.

"large" and "small," "round" and "square" and color names often, he soon comes to link these names to the right toy.

Sorting things
You can point out all sorts of similarities and differences to your child and let him practice classifying and sorting various things. Any odd assortment of objects that are big enough, at least 1½in (4cm) in all dimensions, and safe for him to handle can be given to him to sort in his own particular way.

Playing sorting games with him helps him to work out which names fit which objects and that some things are more alike than others. A heap of toy farm animals can be fun for him to sort out into whatever categories he chooses. Later you can show him that some are cows, some are pigs, some are horses and with your help he may be able to sort them into different animal groups.

You can have a treasure hunt when you're out walking and gather interesting bits that are suitable for sorting – large pebbles, pine cones, leaves, feathers, chestnuts. When you get home you can sort them out together.

Learning more about shapes

At this age, your child may take great pleasure in rolling a ping pong ball through a cardboard tube and he may have found that a bigger ball or block won't fit at all. He is learning about "smaller" and "larger" and that some shapes fit together while others don't.

Simple shape sorters may be more understandable to him now as he comes to match the shape in his hand with the opening in the top. You can make the simplest sorter for him by cutting a round shape the size of a ping pong ball and a square the size of a block in the top of a shoebox. You can show him how sorters work if you hold the shape above the hole, and let him push it through. He will gain a sense of achievement, especially if you praise him for doing so well and he will soon get the idea. Some sorters also have color-coding, so that the red shape fits into the red slot. You can

Your child's first interest in a toy train may be to master how it links together. Then he may take it apart and put it together over and over again.

show this to him, and he may understand matching colors, though true color recognition may come later.

First puzzles

From around his first birthday, when his interest in objects is intense, your child may begin to play with the pieces of puzzles. The first to introduce are inset boards or playtrays, with simple shapes and colors. These are the easiest for him to use and may have the basic shapes that are found in a shape sorter. Other playtrays have a theme like farm animals or different kinds of vehicles. The pieces often stand up by themselves and he can see how they relate to each other and to the tray they fit into. Each piece usually has a little peg to lift it out and fit it back into place. Some have pictures under the shapes and this makes them even more attractive. If you show your child how the shapes match the wells in the tray, he soon gets the idea of fitting them back in.

Fitting pegs in holes is another favorite occupation; cars or other vehicles with spaces for "peg-people" may start to be of interest now.

Playtrays, inset boards, shape sorters and blocks help your child to organize things and make connections between them.

Books and rhymes

things in it. Large format books which show objects and words in different categories such as in the kitchen, on the farm or at the building site, help to increase his vocabulary and understanding.

Simple stories are popular at this age and he may well want to hear the same one again and again. He will soon "know" the sequence and surprise you at the amount he remembers.

Novelty books

Books which involve the child in various ways are very successful. Ones which squeak when he presses the picture, books with flaps which lift up to reveal a hidden object underneath, or books in which things pop up stimulate his interest. Books that he likes get a lot of use and robust ones, at this stage, will last longest. Those made of cardboard or very stiff paper are best because they are strong and the pages are easy to turn, and ones with a glossy surface can be wiped clean.

Books to enjoy anytime

If your toddler is one who wakes early in the morning, books in his crib are an excellent idea. Only put in those that won't tear easily as your child will have plenty of opportunity to shred them unobserved! Books are invaluable as entertainment when you go on long journeys or have to wait at a bus stop or in the doctor's office.

A book at bedtime is a traditional and wonderful way

By looking at books from an early age your child learns to link the pictures in the book with familiar objects around him. He may sometimes have difficulty knowing which is real; you may find him trying to pick a picture of a cookie out of a book or open a door he sees on a page.

A real appreciation of books begins to show itself at this age, particularly if you have spent time reading with your child as a baby. Now, sitting with him and looking at books, pointing things out and talking about the pictures is even more rewarding for you both. Simple books with bold, clear illustrations, often showing ordinary household objects, animals and people are the most popular. By his second birthday more complex illustrations with lots of detail are of interest. You can spend a long time over each page looking at all the different

I hear thunder, I hear thunder,
Hark don't you, hark don't you?
Pitter patter raindrops, pitter
patter raindrops, I'm wet
through. So are you!

Stamp to make thundery noises
or drum fingers on the table.
Put hand to ear. Wiggle fingers
to indicate raindrops then point
to yourself and to your child.

One, two, three, four, five;
Once I caught a fish alive.
Six, seven, eight, nine, ten,
Then I let him go again.
Why did you let him go?
Because he bit my finger so.
Which finger did he bite?
This little finger on your right.

Count the child's fingers, mime
catching the fish and letting it
go, pretend to bite the child's
finger and wiggle it.

Incy Wincy Spider
Climbed up the water spout.
Down came the rain, and
washed the spider out.
Out came the sun, and dried
up all the rain, and the Incy
Wincy Spider climbed up the
spout again!

Walk your fingers up in the air
or on your child like a spider.
Mimic raindrops coming down
and make an action of washing
water away. Draw the sun in the
air, and then the spider coming
up again.

to unwind at the end of the day
and spend some warm and
comfortable moments with
your child. Reading to him is a
quiet activity which helps him
to relax and helps you both to
feel close at the end of the day.
If, when you've finished, you
leave the book with him to look
at, he has a bridge which allows
him to let go of you more easily.

Nursery rhymes
Books of nursery rhymes and
traditional songs delight a
young child, especially when
you sing them together.

**Some books go on fascinating your
child for a long time, especially if
they actively involve him by
folding out, popping up, having
flaps to pull or wheels to roll.**

Children of this age love action
songs when they can join in.
Above are some favorites.

Messy play

Messy play is hugely enjoyable and satisfying in itself as well as giving a child of this age the essential opportunity to experiment with and explore substances like sand, water, playdough or clay. It is an outlet for him to express himself and leads to creative play of all kinds. Some children are hesitant about making a mess and need to be encouraged to let go; others need to be watched if the mess is not to spread all over the house. If you are anxious about messy play, find a time when you won't be hurried and can enjoy organizing the preparations and cleaning up, as well as taking part.

Playdough is enjoyable and satisfying for a young child to play with. It can be handled in many ways – squeezed, pulled, pressed flat and rolled into a ball, worm, sausages or snakes.

Make the rule that an apron or overall must be worn before allowing play to begin. An old shirt or blouse on backwards with sleeves cut down or an older child's T-shirt which is no longer in use will do as long as it is comfortable and doesn't get in the way. Don't expect these sessions to last too long. Thirty minutes is a very long time for a toddler!

Fun with playdough
Although you can buy playdough in little tubs in different colors, it's easy and quite cheap to make your own.

Long-lasting playdough
8oz plain flour
4oz salt
2 tblsp cream of tartar
1 tblsp vegetable oil
8fl oz water
few drops food coloring

Mix all ingredients except the coloring to make a smooth paste. Put in a saucepan and cook slowly over low heat, stirring occasionally, until the dough comes away from the pan and makes a smooth ball. Remove the dough and when cool add a few drops of food

Sand is quite amazing. It pours when it's dry, but still holds its shape if patterns are drawn in it. When it's wet, it can be packed and molded into different shapes.

coloring, if using, then knead; soak the pan right away. The dough should last for a month or two in an airtight container in the fridge.

If you don't want the trouble of cooking the dough, you can make uncooked dough with 1lb plain flour, 8oz salt, 8fl oz cold water, 1 tblsp of vegetable oil and a few drops of food coloring. Mix all the ingredients except the coloring together to form a ball. Add a few drops of coloring and knead well. Store it in the fridge, in an airtight container. Uncooked playdough will keep for a week or two.

To begin with a small child is probably happy getting the feel of the dough, pulling it apart and patting it. You can make little animals or other shapes for him and as his skills develop he may manage simple things like a sausage, worm or an egg.

If you're making pastry or bread, you can always involve your child. Give him some dough to roll out, pat and knead and you can pop it in the oven with yours.

Play with water and sand
Bathtime gives most children the opportunity to play with water. Make bathtime early enough to give your child time to play before he is too tired.

If you prefer, your child can sit in an empty bath next to a plastic tub full of water. He must still be supervised, but in this way can play with water when it's not "bathtime." His play with water may be quite imitative at this age – "washing up" stacking cups and yogurt pots or bathing dolls and other plastic toys. Sponges to squeeze dry and fill up again are also fun.

Sand, too, can be confined to a small space for indoor play. A small amount in a plastic tub can be dug and mixed with water for mounding or molding into cakes or it can be smoothed and drawn in with fingers or a small rake.

Once you've provided the water and a safe place for your child to play, he will love finding out what water does.

47

Crayons and paints

Your child may enjoy you drawing pictures for her, especially if you draw simple things that she can recognize like a house, a cat, a snail or a mouse. You can do simple drawings of people or pets, naming what you've drawn. You can even make up little stories about your drawings.

Like so many activities at this age, imitation is a strong feature of your child's initial attempts at coloring or painting. When you try to write he may try to grab the pen from you and make marks himself.

First drawing
With these first scribbles he is expressing himself and being creative. He may start cautiously, using a small corner of the paper. Later, as his confidence grows, he may fill up a whole sheet. Although he'll be too young to make any meaningful shapes himself, he will enjoy the idea of drawing things and will be encouraged to try out more scribbles.

Give him crayons for these first drawings. Always buy non-toxic wax crayons, since they often get chewed in the early days, and buy chunky ones which are easy to hold and difficult to break. Ones that produce bright colors without too much pressure being needed as well are the most satisfying for this age. Non-toxic, washable felt tips give added variety to his drawing and produce bright, lively colors. Although they should be used with supervision, they are easy to use and the dramatic results will be greatly appreciated. Pencils are dangerous if your toddler runs around with them in his mouth

48

A child's first scribbles are made with backwards and forwards movements. To do this requires muscle control and coordination of his hand and eyes. As he gains more control, his scribbling becomes individual lines that begin and end. With even more control he produces curved lines or circular shapes.

or jabs at other children with them so make sure you supervise their use.

Painting
Your toddler's first painting sessions give him an opportunity to explore the feel and effects of paint, a new and exciting creative experience. Finger paints are the easiest for this age group to manage.

Start your child off using one color first then let him see what happens when different colors get mixed together. You can also give him pieces of sponge, perhaps cut into shapes, to smear the paint around. Show him the different effects you get from dabbing and dragging with the sponge. If he doesn't mind paint on his hands, or as a way to get him used to the feel of it, you can show him how to make prints with his fingers and hands.

Towards the time of his second birthday your child may be able to hold and use a brush. A chunky brush is the easiest to handle. He can use finger paints with this or you can mix powder paints yourself or provide ready mixed paints, thickened with flour if necessary. Special plastic paint cups with firmly fitting lids are the safest for preventing spills. An easel with newspaper underneath is a good place to paint or you can cover a table with paper.

A place to draw
Some children love scribbling and will do so anywhere – in books, on walls, or on furniture. To help prevent this from happening, make a corner where you keep paper, crayons and washable felt tips within your child's reach so that he can draw whenever he wants and doesn't feel he has to resort to a pen or felt tips on the wallpaper or furniture.

Large sheets of cheap paper or newspaper are fine for your child's first paintings.

Your child's progress

During the time between his first and second birthdays your child develops from a baby into a toddler. His first independent steps, first words and first imaginative games usually occur now and his personality becomes more clearly defined. He understands more than he can say and can show that he knows where his things are kept. He also knows the names for parts of his body. Skills with his hands improve enabling him to start to make things himself.

Control of his body

During this year your child learns to walk and run and by 18 months he can probably walk up steps unaided. By two he may be able to climb up and down steps and stairs and onto furniture. He loves to push, pull and ride on things and will be able to scoot along with his feet. As his physical skills develop he becomes more assured and confident.

Control of his hands

In this year your child learns to put shapes in holes, build a tower of several blocks, fit objects into one another and turn things in a screw-like motion. By 18 months your toddler will be able to make marks on paper with a pen and his aim when hammering pegs is more accurate. He enjoys kneading pastry or dough and pouring water and sand.

Learning to talk

By 18 months your child is likely to understand quite a number of simple words and often tries to copy the names you use for objects. If he can't yet speak much he will indicate what he wants quite clearly in other ways. He can understand a great deal of what is said to him, and he will be able to obey some commands. Soon he will string words together.

Social skills

Although your two-year-old will still be dependent on his mother he will have developed much closer relationships with other family members or carers with whom he spends a lot of time. He becomes more interested in other children but still just plays alongside them. He is more confident with new people and also remembers much more.

Understanding his world

From about the age of 18 months your child may seem to make enormous leaps in his understanding. He begins to play in a much more purposeful way, imitating you and trying to do and construct things deliberately. He begins to think and plan ahead and is more aware of the outcome of his actions. By two, he begins to grasp ideas of color and shapes.

Here goes

During this year your child becomes more sociable, articulate and better coordinated. She needs toys and games that complement and extend these skills and enable her to understand her world and her place in it. She'll love things that let her pretend to be grown up: tea sets, play houses, props for make-believe games. Playing these games encourages her to speak and use her rapidly expanding vocabulary. Her hand and finger control are also improving and this, together with her wider understanding and imagination, means that she can now begin to make pictures and models and to create a fantasy world with her toys. She still needs new experiences, lots of praise and encouragement and the chance to try out these new skills on her own, with you, and with other children – of whom she becomes increasingly aware. However, she will have times when she wants to do more than she is capable of, which she may find frustrating. She needs you as a secure base from which she can explore her world.

Practical play

Your child's first efforts at building will be quite simple. Using blocks or stacking construction toys or bristle blocks, she may start by making low walls or small towers. At first, it is just the making that's important – what it's meant to be comes later. As the year goes on, these shapes take on an imaginative identity – they represent houses, cars and so on.

If the pieces are too small for her to manage she will soon be discouraged. A system you can add to has the most potential to "grow" with your child. Those which include people, animals and vehicles stimulate a child to use her imagination in building things and extend the life of such construction toys considerably.

Another practical skill that a child of this age may enjoy is threading. Large beads or empty spools are the best to start and shoe laces are easier to use than string. Fine finger movements are exercised as she strings the beads together.

Many toddlers enjoy playing with huge – 12in (30cm) or larger – light blocks to build towers. These can be made simply by taping the lids onto shoe boxes or other cardboard boxes or by filling paper bags with crumpled newspaper, cutting off the handles and taping them closed. Just three blocks will make a tower as tall as a child – and what fun it is to build it and knock it over again!

Building with a purpose
Imaginative play and construction skills can be combined in a wooden or plastic railroad system where

Large interlocking blocks which click together and come apart without too much effort are the easiest for a child of this age to handle. They can be stacked together and later made into even more satisfying constructions such as cars and bridges.

the pieces are fitted together. Some trains come as part of a range of construction kits, others come on their own. Many children enjoy putting these together but will need your help and guidance to begin with. You can add more features such as bridges, tunnels, turntables and stations to make the train set even more enjoyable. This is fun on its own and also a toy to grow with. A playmat also makes a good background for your child to build and play on. She

Toys that look like the real thing may satisfy some would-be carpenters and builders.

can use the mat as a basis for building walls, adding houses, bridges, animal pens or parking lots. These don't have to be elaborate for her to run cars or trains on the roads and under the bridges.

"Help" with repairs

Your toddler will probably be fascinated by any building, repairing or other work going on around the house. If she sees you making or repairing something, her desire to copy you may be overwhelming. She has developed her building skills, using her hands together and may feel she's ready to

A playmat you have made can include features your child recognizes – your house, the park, schools and local shops – which adds to the fun.

take on jobs she sees you doing. A tool kit, with strong wooden or plastic tools robust enough to stand up to real use, can provide hours of pleasure for a toddler. Some kits have a worktop into which pegs can be hammered and screws and nuts turned, allowing her to practice her skills.

Some children seem to become almost obsessed with tools and carry them round the house "fixing" things. You need to be extra watchful and make sure your child can't poke anything, especially

metal, into a plug socket or electrical equipment.

You can try providing her with her own pieces of safe equipment or toy vehicles to fix and set aside a time when you can guide and supervise her play. Make it very clear to her that some things are hers to use, but others are not. If she has plenty of opportunities to use tools that she enjoys and that she can play with safely, she is more likely to cooperate when you ask her not to "repair" the television!

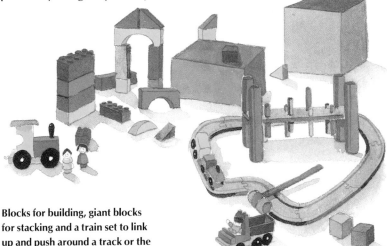

Blocks for building, giant blocks for stacking and a train set to link up and push around a track or the floor are all toys that fascinate a child now.

A world of make-believe

At this age a child is learning to sort out and organize his world. One way he does this is to play games that imitate what he sees you do, with his toys taking on new roles.

From the age of about two your child will use her imagination more and more to animate toys and objects and will enjoy playing with miniature people, such as the "peg people" that fit into toys, the plastic figures which come with some construction kits or little dolls which fit into dolls' houses. The ones with moveable limbs are especially enjoyable.

An assortment of miniature people and animals can be used in many different games.

At first she will use them in the setting they came in, then, gradually, she will use her imagination to create other games with them. She may make some kind of "house" to put them in, some vehicles to drive them around in, and one or two other props like "food" for them to eat. A cardboard box and other odd bits may be enough for some children to create the scene for all kinds of involved games. Other children need more obvious props and your suggestions about what can be used to represent various things. Small plastic animals are very popular, too, although at this age they may take on various uses, not the "role" you expect.

Pretend play

Your child may use miniature toy people or her dolls and soft toys to act out scenes from everyday life as well as major events. She may also use them to show her feelings – she may tell off one of the characters or send one away, or get one of the other toys to smack one.

She will be delighted if you join in with these games, but it's important to remember how real they are to her. She may become very upset if you spoil the game by making a "person" act in a way which she hasn't planned for, so it is important to let her take the lead.

Puppets are also fascinating toys that come to life and are particularly good for encouraging your child to speak. You can make a puppet easily out of an old sock or mitten, sewing or sticking on beads or buttons for eyes and a nose, felt for a tongue, and adding ears and a woolly mop for hair. Simpler still, you can draw a face on a plain paper bag and she can either place it over her hand, or you can fill it with crumpled paper and put it over a cardboard tube, then gather in the bottom of the bag with an elastic band.

Finger puppets are fun too and help to develop finger and hand control. You can make them from felt or paper. Make them large enough to fit over

A large hat, shoes, a handbag, small case or shopping bag or basket are all a child needs for early imaginative play.

the finger but still allow the finger to bend. Your child can use them to act out favorite stories and nursery rhymes.

Dressing up
As well as entering a make–believe world in miniature with her dolls, your child may enjoy dressing up. At first such games will be quite simple, copying games, reflecting what she sees around her. She may dress up or use certain props and, perhaps, play house. You can start a dressing up box into which you can put old clothes, hats, jewelry, flat-heeled shoes and other useful props. She might like to pretend she's "going shopping" or "going on vacation." She can choose a few items to pack in a small case such as a plastic lunch-box or an old handbag. You can attach a luggage label with her name and/or picture on it and she can then "depart" into another room or the garden.

Chairs can be clever props too: in a row to represent a train, facing each other to make a boat, or in a circle with a sheet draped over to become a tent, den or cave.

Playing with others
Although children of two to three show signs of playing together, and they may carefully assign roles – "You be the daddy" – most of their play is still side by side and they are unable to cooperate for long. They do, however, enjoy playing with older children, perhaps seeing them as adults. Games of house, with children of their own age, may keep them playing together for a while, but you may notice that each child is "doing their own thing" within the game. You will need to supervise such games when children play together and intervene quite often to make peace, suggest other options, oversee taking turns, or finding another equally desirable hat or garment if one child feels left out. If you plan to keep these first encounters short they will be more successful. You may also find that if your child becomes very possessive and unwilling to share her toys, that everyone will be happier in a neutral place – such as the park or playground.

Puppets are easy to make and excellent for encouraging speech development. Your child can take many parts in a puppet show.

Puzzles and games

Puzzles and games help your child to understand how things are ordered and grouped. Puzzles, especially, can be very absorbing. Your child may study each piece carefully, working out visually where it

You can make simple two, three or four piece puzzles for her by gluing easily recognized pictures – faces, cars, animals – cut out of magazines – to cardboard and cutting them out into jigsaw shapes. Your child will be delighted to put the picture together again. You can also make several puzzles with straight edges so she can assemble them in any unusual way she likes.

Understanding numbers

Puzzles give you a good chance to talk to your child about the picture in the puzzle, the shapes and colors of the pieces and how some pieces almost fit together but only one is just right. Or if there are two gaps left, it takes two pieces to fill them. She may begin to relate the names for numbers she has heard in nursery rhymes or as you counted when climbing up the stairs with her to real objects.

At first children tend to understand only three

You can make a simple fishing game together and at first just catch the "fish." Later you can count them or sort them by shape or color.

fits into the whole. She may still enjoy inset boards and playtrays and may be ready, during this year, to move on to jigsaws with a few large pieces that fit into a clearly defined surround. Start off with jigsaw puzzles of five or six pieces. If you do most of the puzzle and leave her to finish it by fitting in the last piece or two, she'll have the satisfaction of completing the puzzle without getting frustrated at trying to do a task that may be too difficult for her.

Your child may need help at first with puzzles, but enjoys putting the pieces in if you show her where they go.

numbers – one, two and "lots" or "too many." While she may rattle off a string of numbers, like "one-two-three-four-five", she is unlikely to understand what they mean. Big and little, lots and a few or only one are ideas she can probably understand, though, and the "business" of counting as part of a rhyme may be something she also enjoys.

Counting can be a natural part of your conversation – count her buttons as you do up her coat, count her toes as you dry them after a bath. This will get her used to the idea of numbers and things without pushing her to get it right.

A good game to further the idea of numbers and use colors as well is "Fishing." You can buy a ready-made game, but it's easy to make one yourself. Use a box or plastic tub for the pond, and make fish out of cardboard or colored paper with a paper-clip mouth. You can start with two or three fish in two or three different colors. Take a 12in (30cm) long stick or piece of dowelling and tie a piece of string to it with a small magnet tied to the other end. Help your child to start with, and she will soon get the idea of catching the fish and pulling them out. Try making different shapes and colored fish so she can sort them out and put them in piles as they are caught. You can count them together when all the fish have been brought in.

Language and understanding

Playing games like "Fishing" gives you a chance to talk about colors. At this age she may match identical colors even if she isn't sure of their names and practicing using them will help her to understand what the different names mean. Casually mention the different colors of blocks, pictures in a book, her clothes and toys. Toys that feature color matching can be helpful too; a red key which fits into a red door, or a red shape which fits into a square red hole, while only a blue shape fits into a round blue hole, will help her to recognize and match the colors with the shapes.

Sorting and matching things are still favorite activities at this age, whether it's sorting out her blocks according to color, or finding two alike among her toys or the foods in the cupboard. At this age, picture lotto is a good game to introduce. Since the picture is always there, she doesn't have to remember it, but she can match it. Near the age of three, she may be ready for a simplified game like "Snap," played without cards. Each child has an assortment of small objects – toy animals, small blocks, toy cars, buttons and such – and they produce one object at the same time from the pile. The "winner" is the one who shouts "Snap" if they show the same object.

Another game which children of this age begin to enjoy is picture dominoes. At first they will enjoy recognizing the pictures; then the idea of matching and putting them in line will appeal. Help your child to look for the next domino and gain the satisfaction of making a nice long line.

A pegboard game can be fun and encourages your child to observe and concentrate. You make a line of different colored pegs and get her to copy the pattern. Start by alternating two colors at first, then add more if she copies yours easily. Or you can use threading beads to make a sequence for her to copy.

Picture lotto and floor puzzles help a child to observe and concentrate. Pop-up toys are useful for color matching.

Using cushions as trampolines for bouncing is a lot of fun and helps children to develop strong leg muscles as well as have a great time together.

Active play

Active, physical play both indoors and out is vital to children especially now. Your child has lots of energy to use up as she develops her coordination and physical skills. She gains confidence and independence too, as she perfects her jumping, climbing and throwing.

Active play indoors
Children don't stop being active just because it's raining and if they're warm and well protected they will really love playing in the rain and splashing in puddles. The air feels different in the rain and the variety of experiencing it will be fun. However, when outdoor play is impossible one good way of working off excess energy is trampolining. A big cushion or old mattress, as long as it's not ripped, that you can store under a bed makes an ideal trampoline. Keep it away from any furniture with sharp corners and put some pillows or cushions on the floor to break a fall. You will need to supervise the activity and remember that two or more children bouncing together can easily collide or bang their heads together; making a rule to take turns may help. Some music to bounce in time to can make trampolining even more fun.

A smooth board with sanded edges makes a ramp to roll things down. A tray or a hardboard offcut would also do. It can be propped up on the lower rung of a chair, the edge of a stool, sofa or step. Balls, toy cars and trucks or any wheeled vehicles can be rolled down the ramp or it can be a slide for dolls and teddies. Different objects will move at different rates and some will roll better than others.

A plank supported on books at each end makes a raised board to walk along, for practicing her "tightrope" walking and improving her balance. You can also make an indoor obstacle course that consists of a tunnel of chairs and boxes to crawl through, stepping stones made of a sheet of newspaper, a raised walkway and a blanket to crawl under. Or you could suggest that the floor is water or molasses and place newspaper or magazine islands down that she has to move around on without touching the floor.

Hiding games are always fun, if you take it in turns to hide and try to find each other. Or, have a treasure hunt, where you make a list of objects for your child to find. You can show her as you tick them off as she finds them. You can send your child on an "errand" to get one item, then try sending her for two different things. This improves both her memory and her concentration.

"Simon Says" is an excellent indoor game for learning parts of the body and to encourage listening. Only commands that begin "Simon says" are to be obeyed. Anyone who does something that does not start "Simon Says" is out.

Indoors and out
Sit-and-ride toys and pushalongs also encourage lively physical play. Wheeled vehicles of different designs – lorries, fire-engines with firemen and a hose, tractors or other kinds of vehicle – may capture her imagination. If you haven't room in the house for her to get up any speed, take the toy out for a trip round the

A child enjoys copying your actions – jumping, walking backwards, spinning round, holding arms out and so on. She patterns her movements on yours and masters them in time.

block or to the park.

Ball games, too provide her with a chance to run as well as helping her to learn to kick, throw and to try to catch. These activities help to refine hand and eye coordination. Outdoors, you can use a large ball to encourage your child to run and kick. Indoors, a

A ramp can be a slide for a doll, and a place to find out that things roll at different speeds and some don't roll at all.

smaller, lighter ball can still be used for her to roll, throw and chase. A light plastic ball with holes in it or a ping pong ball are the safest indoors.

A beach ball or under-inflated balloon may be easier for a two-year-old to throw and hit or bat with her hand. Then, as her skills develop, she can use balls which are smaller and heavier. Rolling a ball to you is easiest for her at first. At this age, when she actually tries to throw, she tends to stand with her feet together and throw the ball downwards in a clumsy movement.

Kicking is also difficult at first, but a skill she may well acquire during this year. At first she may simply walk or run into a ball, pushing it forward, then she learns to take her weight on one leg while she swings the other to kick.

Talking and understanding

During this year a child may begin to see books as more than a series of pictures; she begins to appreciate stories too and likes to share them with her friends – often exactly as she has heard you read them.

From the age of two your child's vocabulary grows and she begins putting words together in two- or three-word phrases. Gradually she uses more words and then whole sentences. She can explain to you much more clearly both what she wants and what she is thinking. Playing helps language growth and expressive skills by encouraging her to talk about what she's doing.

Looking at books
Books are often a child's great love at this age. As well as wanting to look at the pictures, she'll listen as you read her a story and, as the year goes on,

she'll be able to cope with more detailed stories.

When choosing books for her, look for those with large, attractive pictures, with a lot of detail in them. They may or may not have a simple story-line which she can follow. Books which repeat part of the story or have a refrain in them are often very popular.

From the age of two your child may also like stories which rhyme, as the rhymes help her to guess what is coming next, and also make it easier to remember the story next time. You may find you are asked to read the same story over and over again, even if you are tired of it! And if you get a word wrong or leave out a part you will be told quite adamantly what it should be.

Books can be useful for learning other skills too, such as numbers, colors, shapes and sizes. Counting books and alphabet books may appeal to a child of this age, but she's just as likely to learn from the books she already has if you talk about "how many" and "what color" while she looks on and follows. She may also start to recognize some letters if they're displayed prominently on the page.

The library
Visiting your local library can be an outing for you both and you can borrow a variety of books to see which your child likes best. If she has her own

A child understands much more than she can put into words, and begins to make herself understood, combining gestures with a single word, like "Juice" when she wants a drink. She then progresses to simple phrases. As she nears three years of age, she wants to find out as much as she can about herself and her world and learns to ask "What's that?" and "Why?" She wants to know more words and the more words she knows, the more quickly she can think. Answer her briefly and clearly, in terms she can understand to increase her vocabulary and help her language development.

library card as well, she will feel very important and grown up, especially if she helps to choose her own books and has them checked in and out.

Storytelling

Stories needn't always come from books, of course. You may find your child likes listening to stories which you can tell her at bedtime, or while waiting for a bus or to see the doctor. Lying down on the bed with your child, closing your eyes and telling a story can be a wonderful way for you both to get a rest during the day if she has dropped her daytime nap. You may remember stories you enjoyed as a child or repeat stories from her favorite books. The stories she may enjoy most, though, are ones you make up based on her own experience, personal stories about what she knows and recognizes. You

can weave in her friends into her own personal adventures.

Talking together

Children absorb a lot by looking, listening and repeating, without you making an obvious effort to "make" them learn. For this reason, talking to your child continues to be very important and will help her to develop her vocabulary and communication skills. It's important to keep up a steady flow of conversation that relates to what she's

A child will love it when you point things out and talk to him about what he can see and hear. When you're out walking, keep up a running commentary as you walk along.

doing. Give her time too to take part in the conversation. She may make lots of mistakes in making sounds and putting her words together, but rather than correcting her, which may undermine her confidence, give her a good model and she'll catch on before long.

Word games

Besides delighting her, word games encourage her to speak up and practice her vocabulary. Make up silly rhymes such as: "This little piggy went to town/ this little piggy fell down/this little piggy bumped his head/ this little piggy went to bed/ And this little piggy wore a crown." This gets her used to the rhythm of language and the idea that you can change it and play and have fun with it.

Play negative games such as: "What's Susie wearing? Is it pajamas? Is it sausages? Is it . . ." Before you've finished, she may burst out, "No, it's a hat!"

Making music

Most young children enjoy listening to music, singing, dancing or making music. It involves their minds and bodies and can help in learning to speak as well as providing good opportunities to practice listening and paying attention. It's also great fun and an excellent way to tell them that it's all right to be noisy and let off steam.

Your child's first introduction to music was probably nursery rhymes and songs you sang to her as a baby. As she gets older, she may start to sing the tunes to herself when playing quietly or when she's in bed. You can sing along with her and teach her new rhymes and songs, and also some action rhymes which she will enjoy.

Simple musical instruments give her a chance to try using

Anyone can make music. Children can have a great time playing instruments as they march along to music they make themselves or "playing" along with the radio or a record or cassette.

An assortment of instruments gives your child the chance to experience lots of ways of making different sounds. Many instruments can be made from everyday materials.

different skills. A whistle or simple recorder or pipe will help her learn how to blow and produce a noise; a tambourine can be used as a drum to thump and it jangles as well; a xylophone plays different notes and helps her to listen for the different sounds that she can make it produce.

A saucepan or a plastic food container with a lid makes a simple drum and a wooden spoon an easy drumstick; saucepan lids can be cymbals; small pasta shapes, dried peas or sand securely sealed in a plastic jar or bottle make excellent maracas. Metal objects hung on strings and struck with a metal spoon are simple chimes and you can always find a use for a baby's rattle as a rhythm instrument.

Your child becomes aware of different rhythms by hearing instruments played slowly and quickly, and you can show her the difference between loud and soft sounds too. This encourages her to listen and try to imitate what you're doing. Ask her to make a loud noise like an elephant or a small squeak like a mouse and she'll find out that she can make soft and loud noises too.

Let's dance and sing
Making music is a good social activity when you have another child or children of the same age over to play. Sit them in a group and they will probably have great fun playing and making a noise together.

Moving to music encourages your child to listen and associate what she is hearing with what she's doing. Children's songs often give instructions for clapping or moving in some specific way, but you can just turn on the radio for music to move to. You may have to start the play as a

Here are some songs and action rhymes your child might enjoy:

Put your finger on your ear, on your ear, (Repeat)
Put your finger on your ear,
Leave it there about a year,
Put your finger on your ear, on your ear.

Put your finger on your head, on your head, (Repeat)
Put your finger on your head,
Tell me is it green or red,
Put your finger on your head, on your head.

You can make up verses for this indefinitely and it's good for learning parts of the body. Some suggestions:

Put your finger on your cheek, Leave it there about a week.

Put your finger on your nose, Leave it there until it snows.

Jack-in-the-box jumps in the air, He makes me laugh as he wriggles his head.
I gently press him down again, Saying Jack-in-the-box you must go to bed.

Sit with your child in front of you. Lift her up in the air and wriggle her, then press gently to make her curl up again.

Heads, shoulders, knees and toes, knees and toes (Repeat)
And eyes and ears and mouth and nose,
Heads, shoulders, knees and toes, knees and toes.

Point to the different parts of the body.

"follow the leader" game and move in ways that suit the music – galloping, marching, swaying, jumping, swinging arms, flexing fingers. Or you can dance together as partners holding hands – or holding her.

It's probably worth buying a cassette or two with good songs for young children to sing. Some of these have more than the traditional nursery rhymes and are especially popular if sung by children. They often have actions that go with them and encourage listening skills. They can be very useful to help pass the time if you're going on a long car journey too.

Picture making

In the year from two to three your child will be able to begin exploring many ways of making pictures. In addition to playing with the texture and colors of paint, felt tips or crayons, she will be interested in putting things together to make a picture or collage, even if it doesn't look like much to you.

Painting techniques

When she is able to handle a brush, she'll enjoy using one for painting. Make sure you protect the floor and other surfaces with newspaper or other protective covering, put an apron or smock on your child and, if possible, use non-spill containers for the paint. If you mix powder paints thickly they will be more satisfying to use because they cover the paper better and the colors are more intense. They also make less mess and fewer drips. You can add flour as you mix powder paint, to make it thicker, or let your child use finger paints with a brush.

You can suggest ways to vary the kinds of pictures your child makes with paint too. You can do drip painting by making the paint runny and letting her drip it onto the paper and then holding the paper up, or drop small blobs of paint on the paper and show her how to blow them with a straw.

To make a rainbow painting, "paint" a sheet of paper with water, and then let your child paint lines of color across it or draw lines with washable felt tips; the colors will spread into a lovely rainbow.

She can use other household objects to print with: corks, empty spools, clothes pins, corrugated cardboard and a comb all make interesting patterns. She'll also still enjoy finger painting and making prints with her fingers and hands, so you can end a painting session by making finger and hand prints if her hands are messy from using a brush or printing.

Remember that your child may have a very short concentration span. You may get everything ready, then find she paints two lines on the paper, says she's made a picture of an elephant and wanders off. Don't be discouraged; give her a chance to try again and you may find she's more than willing. Sometimes it helps to have another child of the same age over to visit so that they can paint together, but you will

Your child can now probably handle a short brush and make clearer strokes when painting. Printing with a sponge is also easy to do and gives interesting and varied results.

need to have two of everything if it's not to end in tears.

Using scissors and glue
Your child will have fun cutting and sticking, too. It is not easy to master the art of using scissors and cutting. It calls for a good pair of round-ended scissors and lots of practice. At first, cutting is a pleasure in itself, so let her cut strips of thin card, then go on to cutting shapes out of Christmas or birthday cards. At first she won't be able to cut around shapes, but she enjoys trying.

The shapes can then be stuck down with non-toxic glue. PVA glue is the best to use since it is non-toxic and easy to clean off with cold water. Avoid those glues which give off dangerous fumes or are meant for purposes other than gluing paper. You may find glue sticks are easiest for some play, like sticking bits of paper to cardboard.

Put sheets of paper on the table and help your child to

Glitter, cotton wool, tea leaves, pasta shapes, feathers – all can be used for sticking.

glue things down, spreading the paste with spatulas. To begin with, smearing the glue and seeing that things stick to it is fun enough. She can make pictures by sticking on other things, too: pasta shapes, crumpled kitchen foil, seeds, drinking straws and scraps of fabric all work well. Children love glitter but tend to use it all up at once, so they need to be supervised. However she can make a picture with glue and a substitute for glitter like fine sand, dried coconut or tea leaves to shake over the paper

and stick to the glue. If the glue is put on in squiggles and dribbles she can sprinkle things on it and see that they only stick to the glue, when the excess is tipped off. (This can be saved.)

At this age your child will put many household objects to good use. Cardboard tubes from toilet and kitchen rolls, cardboard egg boxes and other boxes and containers can all be cut up and glued to make animals, people, hats, cars, planes, telescopes and rockets. Your child will enjoy the making process just as much as the end product, so don't be too fussy about how it looks or worried about even giving it a name or identifying what it is.

You can keep a box in the kitchen to collect useful things for her junk sticking and modelling. Straws, corks, dried leaves, silver paper, beads, cellophane, wool and scraps of material can all be added.

Quite splendid collages can be made from ordinary household materials. You can draw outlines for your child to fill in or let her imagination guide her in making her own pictures or abstract designs.

Your child's progress

This year sees your child progress from a willful, often clumsy toddler to a longer-limbed, more graceful and controlled child. Her use of language develops as she begins to speak in phrases, then in whole sentences. As her ability to communicate improves, her play becomes more complex, with more make-believe and "let's pretend" games. Playing with other children also becomes important and she begins to share and take turns.

Control of her body

By about two and a half your child will probably be able to run, jump up and down on the ground and on and off things. By three she will be able to balance briefly on one leg, and stand on tiptoe. She can throw a ball with increasing skill and may be starting to learn to catch. She can climb to quite a height on a suitable jungle gym.

Control of her hands

By about two and a half your child may be able to thread a thick string through a reasonably large hole and may be able to do up large buttons or hooks. By three she has good control of a pen and can draw simple pictures. She can hold and use a suitable pair of scissors and can cut paper strips, though not cut out complicated outlines.

Speech

Between the ages of two and three her speech develops very rapidly. Every day, new words come into her vocabulary. She starts using "I" and "you," "my" and "your," and asking questions, usually beginning with "What's that?" then "Why?" She gradually learns to put sentences together in a more adult way and her pronunciation gets much clearer.

Social skills

Your child becomes much more sociable during this year and increasingly enjoys playing with other children her age. She is only just beginning to understand about sharing and encounters with other children will often involve frequent squabbles, needing you to intervene. Although your child becomes more independent, she still needs one-to-one attention.

Imaginative and creative skills

By her third birthday your child may be using her imagination to create new worlds of play and will want to build and make things as well as act out stories and activities with her toys. She will enjoy more complex stories in books. Her imagination may also make her more fearful of the strange or new and she may need reassurance that she is safe.

Taking off

The pre-school child needs every chance to consolidate the basic skills he has gained and also to develop and apply new abilities, especially his creative and imaginative skills. If he does not go to a nursery school or playgroup it is doubly important for him to learn at home, and to mix with other children his own age too. It is now that he must learn to share, take turns, and get along with other children. He does this through playing together in cooperative games. As in the previous year, "let's pretend" games are very important and you should take them seriously, helping if you are asked, to provide the props to make them even more enjoyable. At this age he will find new functions for old toys, using them in different, more creative ways. As he approaches his fifth birthday he is more able to concentrate, so table top activities come to the fore. His understanding makes tremendous strides and he can follow the rules of simple games. His social world may be expanding, too, and he learns to communicate with new adults and children, paving the way for the transition to school and a wider world.

Let's pretend

Between the ages of three and five your child's imagination really takes off. He embarks on cooperative play with other children for the first time and together they enter into a world of make-believe, choosing different roles: mommies and daddies, doctors and nurses, cowboys and Indians. They begin to plan their games for themselves and as time goes on they are able to carry out these plans without needing your constant direction or support. Events that have happened in the immediate past are remembered and events in the future can be looked forward

A toy medical kit with a stethoscope, syringe and bandages will keep the "doctors" and "nurses" busy for ages.

to. These too may be incorporated in their play.

At this stage, children transform everyday objects for use in their imaginary worlds. A bed can be a boat, a blanket draped over chairs makes a house or castle, the space under the stairs is a rocket capsule. Adding some realistic props helps too; a tea set, pots and pans will give those playing "house" something to use, and share. Dolls, teddies and other stuffed toys will become playmates, and be given roles if there are not enough children to play all the parts and you may be roped in too. The youngest ones, in particular, will demand your assistance as the other passenger on the bus, boat or moon rocket. Do spare the time to join in. Your participation gives your child more security and confidence and may speed up the time when he no longer needs you to get involved. And you may find you enjoy yourself too!

Large toys for these imaginary games may often be popular, although expensive and space-consuming. Toy stoves or kitchenettes, ride-on tractors or racing cars may all be enjoyed and some of those big toys bought at a younger age such as a play house or pushcart may continue to give hours of fun. However, children can turn simple items into the things they need with occasional helpful suggestions from you.

Often you can do a lot to help set up a game, making sure that the surroundings are

Both boys and girls need the chance to play energetically and to explore different roles, enabling them to work out their feelings through their games.

change a child's image of himself. Other simple items like an old shirt to make a surgeon's gown or a striped T-shirt for a pirate and some jewelry for a princess will do as well.

Another exciting prop is a mask. Children believe they are instantly transformed when they put one on. However, masks alarm some children, so

safe, calming disagreements over who will be what, organizing the making of special props like a plane or a spaceship and finding the bits and pieces they need. Once the game gets going, you may find yourself redundant until the children are tired and

fretful, when you may need to bring the game to an end.

Cooling off
If your children tend to get involved in very boisterous and aggressive games, distract them with attractive alternatives rather than just forbidding them to play. They could create a fantasy space world of the future or plan what to take and actually pack a case for an imaginary vacation. Directing them away from conflicts can keep play going longer without it escalating as it might if left unsupervised.

Dressing for the part
A few realistic items, like a fireman's hat, a policeman's helmet, a cowboy hat or a nurse's cap, can quickly

Dressing-up clothes and a few props can add to the fun of imaginative games. Old toys may be rediscovered and used in new and different ways.

don't press the idea if your child objects. Face paints may be a good alternative, making instant clowns or animals.

Toys are unisex
Whether your child is a boy or a girl, they will need all kinds of toys to play with. Boys usually get the tractors, cars, trains and cowboy hats, while girls get the dolls, carriages or strollers, toy stoves, beads and bangles. In reality, both sexes enjoy playing with all kinds of toys and need variety in their play and playthings. A girl can work off aggressive feelings with a water-pistol or build a Lego spaceship as well as a boy, and boys enjoy putting a doll into a stroller or making its lunch. "Domestic play" is essential for the development of boys as it is for girls. Both boys and girls need the chance to copy household games and to try out their creative skills, enabling them to work out their feelings through play.

73

Building takes shape

A train set can "grow" with your child as her imaginative play develops and she creates and peoples a make-believe world.

As your child's hand and finger movements become more skillful and his imagination expands, he is ready to try a new range of building toys and activities. Wooden blocks and larger interlocking blocks are less versatile than more intricate construction toys such as Lego, which also have small figures with interchangeable parts to enact different roles and provide lots of fun. Many construction toys come in varying degrees of complexity for different ages, starting out with the basic blocks and figures with non-detachable parts and going on to the smaller and more intricate pieces.

Your child's imaginative play may go beyond his ability to set the scene for his play in a practical way. Let him take the lead in choosing what he wants

to build, being prepared to give help where and when it's needed. He will learn by trial and error that blocks which overlap form a stronger bond than those simply placed one above another and that building anything too high may suddenly collapse.

As you talk about what he is building his vocabulary and understanding can be stretched. More complex shape words like cylinder, cube, and pyramid can be used and understood. Comparatives – taller, smaller, bigger, shorter – and their superlatives – tallest, smallest, biggest and shortest – will also make more sense to him.

Children of four and five, and even older, will still enjoy playing with blocks and toy cars when making props for an imaginative game. Just because they now enjoy making a car from small components does not mean they do not enjoy lining up all their ready-made cars and any others they have to make a traffic jam!

Real building
At this age your child will enjoy outings and visits of all kinds. If there is a construction site nearby, you can visit it together every few days and watch the building grow and change. You can talk about what the men are doing, what machines they are using and how the site has changed from the previous visit. Any experience like this gives your child something to think about and extends his own imitative and imaginative play. It also exercises his memory, improves his powers of observation and increases his vocabulary.

Play people
As well as building houses, vehicles and other structures, your child may like the small figures which go with some construction sets; he will put them in and out of their buildings, into the car or helicopter they came in, and move them around. Other

Some children like abstract construction toys to make unusual and imaginative shapes. Others prefer more conventional interlocking blocks.

small figures have various roles: doctors and nurses, cowboys and Indians, explorers, pirates, and so on. Children seem fascinated by the tiny props that go with them and often play elaborate make-believe games with them.

His wooden building blocks or a train set can be incorporated into his imaginative games. Wooden blocks can be used for the train station and town where the small figures live; you can extend a railroad layout for an older child or bring in other items, such as plastic farm or zoo animals. Again, when you talk to him you can use naturally words that describe the positions of objects – concepts such as on top of, in the middle, left, right, in front of and behind. His understanding will come from

seeing and using the words in the context of his play. He may also give a running commentary of what he is doing as he plays. This helps him to sort out and think about what is happening.

Children often like other, more abstract construction toys. These can be flat pieces of plastic or straws which interlock in various ways and can be used to build all kinds of different shapes and structures which may be incorporated into imaginative play.

Puzzles and jigsaws
Many of the skills that he needs for building, such as planning ahead and hand control, are related to the skills used in doing jigsaws. Your child may be ready for more advanced puzzles now to encourage him to plan ahead and think things through. His problem-solving abilities are also taxed by jigsaws. Not only does he have to look at the picture, he also has to match the shapes and colors of all the pieces and then fit the pieces together.

At this age your child can direct her own imaginative play – even to make a traffic jam.

Making models

As well as still enjoying rolling and kneading playdough and clay, and cutting it out into simple shapes, your child may now begin to use these materials to make a greater variety of different shapes, perhaps an animal, a person, a fruit bowl or a car. He may need larger quantities and different colors to do what he wants with it and perhaps to use some more props as well. A rolling pin and cookie cutters in various shapes will add a new dimension to his fun.

You can also bake playdough in the oven, rather like modelling clay, so that the shapes your child makes can be kept longer.

Clay is also fun at this age, though stiffer and harder to work with than dough. Try to keep the colors separate for as long as possible, as once it's mixed into a greyish blob it loses its appeal and gives less scope for your child's imagination. Start off by letting your child experiment and see what he can do, and find out that the clay gets softer and easier to work as it is used. Later you can make simple things with him such as a ball, sausages, a snake, a snail or a pot. He may try to make complicated objects like a spaceship or a car. These may look nothing like the real thing, but in your child's imagination they will be what he intended. He is showing his natural creativity and needs your encouragement and respect to keep it going.

Cooking

Your child will love being included in helping you with the cooking or baking, trying out his modelling skills on real

Children love to help in the kitchen and cooking uses many of the same skills as playing with playdough or clay, with the added bonus of having something to eat at the end.

Your child may begin to make more elaborate models with clay.

dough or pastry. A baking session with you can be a lot of fun. You can make loaves or buns and let your child help with measuring the ingredients, kneading or rolling the dough or pastry and making different shapes to fix to the top of the loaf. When you are making pastry your child can cut out fish, leaves or other flat shapes to put on top to decorate the pie or he can cut out shapes for cookies.

Children love to make cookies – especially helping to mix all the ingredients or roll out the cookie dough and cut shapes. Making cupcakes is fun too, and your child can spoon the mixture into paper molds and decorate the tops.

Safety in the kitchen

Children in the kitchen must always be supervised at this age. Make clear to them that hands and all work surfaces must be clean before they start. Only adults should use the stove and great care must be taken with knives. Start a child with a blunt knife and a flat board to cut on. A damp cloth under a bowl stops it from slipping as your child mixes.

Hand skills

Wood is another very satisfying material to work with and your child may be attracted to it, particularly if he has seen you making things from wood. You can get tool kits which are suitable for a four-to-five-year-old and which allow him to hammer pieces of soft wood together with large-headed nails. He can also try sanding wood or using a screwdriver. If you do introduce such activities you must be there to supervise at all times.

If your child has watched you sew or mend he may enjoy simple lacing and sewing cards which enable him to practice sewing. They are very good for inspiring fine movements of his fingers as well as his hands.

With some non-toxic glue, paint and imagination your child may want to make models out of many household items. The finished product may not have to be anything at all. Your child may be satisfied simply with the activity, though he will now probably give an object a label if you ask him what it is. Provide your child with a wide assortment of bits and pieces. It's still worth keeping a store of suitable materials for junk modelling so that when he is in the mood you've got plenty of things for him to use. You may need to help with cutting out shapes for him, making things stick together and finding bits that he needs. On the whole a modelling session will be more successful if you let him direct you rather than the other way round. He creates the object in his imagination and you help him to carry it out.

Shoe boxes, plastic containers, egg boxes, cereal packets and the like can be glued together and painted to make all sorts of models.

Cutting and sticking

In the year before school your child's skill in holding and using a pair of scissors and in cutting out shapes may increase enormously. He will now be able to make collages, cut-outs and more adventurous kinds of pictures.

Creative collage
Colored paper is the basis for many of these activities. You can provide tissue paper, wrapping paper, scraps of wallpaper, magazines, old catalogues and old birthday and Christmas cards for your child to use to cut shapes from. Gummed paper stars, dots or other shapes, pieces of wool, bits of fabric left over from dressmaking and pieces of ribbon can all be used by your child to good effect. He can also use dried leaves or flowers from the garden, feathers, cotton balls, pasta shapes, red lentils, glitter or tea leaves. Aluminum foil and flattened drinking straws are useful too.

Safe, non-toxic PVA glue is best for sticking and will be used in large quantities if this is an activity your child enjoys. Glue sticks are also easy to use and neat. If your child uses a liquid glue, put a small amount in a cup and provide a small brush or spatula to spread it.

Collages are easy to do and can look very good if you give your child some help getting started. Together you can draw or cut out a basic shape to use, perhaps an animal or a fish, and let him fill in the detail. Provide bits of flattened drinking straws for the quills of a porcupine, feathers for a bird, aluminum foil for fish scales. The background can also be important; leaves make

At this age children like to have a reason for making things and particularly enjoy making cards and gifts.

a good backdrop for many animals and green and blue tissue paper can be used for a good watery effect.

Sticking without glue
Magnetic and vinyl stick-on-boards and felt shapes with a stick-on background are fun

and safe for your child to use. He can stick the pieces to the background board or scene and make a farmyard or castle come to life. With the sets that consist of abstract shapes he can make interesting and attractive patterns.

While a three-year-old may be happy simply cutting and sticking, and will be pleased with the making rather than concerned with the end result, when he is older, your child will almost certainly want some help and guidance in making a finished product which matches up to his expectations. Although he may still find the activity in itself rewarding, by the age of five he may also have a clear idea in his mind of what he wants to make, and could be very disappointed if he isn't able to achieve it, so he needs

Magnetic, felt, vinyl or stick-on shapes that can be arranged on a paper or board can be especially satisfying for a child who has difficulty using scissors.

some support. However, he may lose interest very quickly if he thinks you're taking over or doing something he feels is too difficult. Letting him make something his own way – or at least go as far as he can – will encourage his creativity and sustain his interest.

Special occasion cards
Children love making cards, especially at Christmas time and for birthdays. He can make simple cards by cutting out shapes like a Christmas tree and then sticking on the decorations. Or he can cut out balloon shapes or simple animals and stick them down. Doing this makes children aware of outlines and shapes.

Scrapbooks
A child of this age may enjoy collecting "special" things which he keeps in a scrapbook. Favorite pictures from magazines, stickers, stamps, post cards, even candy wrappers, can be stuck down.

Other ideas for things to make together:

A whizzer or Catherine wheel
Cut a disc out of card and decorate it. Make two holes in the centre and thread a piece of string or elastic (18in/45cm) through and tie it. Twist the string, then pull outwards to make the disc spin.

A tortoise
Make a cardboard cut-out of a tortoise and glue on pieces of aluminum foil. Pieces of egg shell, especially brown or speckled ones, also make an attractive effect.

A house
Make the front of a house out of card, with windows and doors which hinge open. Glue the house front on top of another piece of paper on which animals, people or another scene have been stuck so that when the windows are opened you can see inside.

Drawing and coloring

Your child's abilities to draw and paint leap ahead in the two pre-school years as both his powers of observation and his muscle control improve.

Your child benefits both from opportunities for free drawing to express his feelings about experiences he has had and to show what he thinks is important, and also from more controlled activities such as drawing around stencils and coloring which help improve his hand and finger control.

The right tools
As his skill at drawing improves, your child may find he wants something better suited to drawing than wax crayons. Washable felt tips which are neither too chunky nor too fine are probably the easiest to handle. When he is drawing, watch how he holds the pen or crayon, as this can make a big difference to his drawing of shapes and later writing. Show him how to hold the pen near the end with his fingers wrapped around it, rather than in a clenched fist at the far end. Large pieces of paper are best if your child is to use his imagination and many children enjoy drawing in a plain book. It can be something that he can keep now that becomes a permanent record of his pictures. He will probably still use crayons for coloring in pictures, although his first efforts may be quite clumsy. Coloring will help him practice fine coordination and exactness – and children do love it. As well as coloring books with pre-printed pictures, he will also enjoy simple activity books with missing bits of outline to be filled in, or pictures outside a frame to be matched with pictures inside a frame. Matching and pattern recognition are useful practice for pre-reading skills.

Stencils and templates
Your child will probably also enjoy making a picture with stencils or templates. You can make your own templates by cutting out figures from thick card, or using household objects such as cookie cutters, or puzzle pieces to draw around. Stencils can be made by cutting a shape out of card and taping the card to a piece of paper so that your child can

Children's drawing follows a common, universal pattern of development, although each child arrives at it himself. Once a round shape is mastered, dots are added for eyes and a nose. Straight lines become arms, usually coming directly from the head. The enlarged head gradually gets smaller and the arms move down, as the legs get longer and enclose a "body." More detail is then added such as fingers, feet, and perhaps the beginnings of clothes and shoes.

Children use drawings to express their feelings about experiences they have had and to show what they think is important.

paint or crayon over it and remove it to see what emerges.

Some templates, leaves, coins, the pavement, car tires and many things can be used for rubbings. Place thin, plain paper over the object and rub with a crayon or pencil.

Painting techniques

As he gets older your child will also enjoy new painting techniques. He can do a painting and fold the paper while the paint is still wet to get a mirror image on each side of the fold. A "magic" painting is fun too. Let him scribble or draw with a white candle on a sheet of paper, then paint over it to see what he's drawn.

Let him mix different colors of paint together to make a range of other distinct colors. From the basic red, yellow and blue he can make purple, orange and green to paint with.

He can do an interesting experiment with color if you pour milk into a shallow bowl or pie plate. Place one drop of food coloring on one side of the bowl, and a drop of a different color on the other. Wait and watch: the effect can be remarkable and quite exciting to a child. When the first result is over, add a few drops of dishwashing liquid and watch the dramatic changes.

Other materials

Different kinds of artists' materials can be experimented with too. Pastel crayons, for example, produce thick, milky colors, going on very easily, and can be deliberately smudged and blended for interesting effects. On black paper these, or chalks, can be used to make a "night-time" picture. Finger paints could be used with wooden popsicle sticks: children love the thickness and texture of these paints, which spike up dramatically to make waves.

Using stencils and templates or abstract painting techniques can help relieve frustration in a child whose free drawing skills may not be very good.

Games

By the age of four most children may like to play simple board or card games. You can make your own "Snap" cards, perhaps with pictures of animals, if you haven't a suitable deck. Snakes and ladders, ludo and other games which involve rolling dice and moving pieces can be fun too, although most children of this age may want to bend the rules if they are losing. Some of them seem to find it very hard to accept losing, so, if he is playing with older children or adults, it may help to let him win sometimes to begin with until he is old enough to understand and accept chance. Losing occasionally though helps him to accept that it is all right to lose too, especially since it is a game he's playing for fun!

Counting the spots on dice can help your child relate numbers and amounts. Magnetic numbers help to show him what numbers look like.

Counting games

Board games can help your child to recognize numbers and learn to count, too. Encourage him to read the dice and see how many squares his piece has to move at each turn. If you haven't got a suitable board game, you can make your own by drawing a course or path with squares to move pieces around it, on a large piece of paper or board, perhaps with various obstacles on the way.

If your child finds it hard to count the dots on small dice, use a plain six-sided wooden cube from his blocks and mark the dots on with a felt tip pen or indelible marker.

Your child can also learn about basic counting through playing shopping games. Use coins or pretend money, and have him count out the right number of coins to pay for the apples, stamps or whatever you are buying from his shop. He can also count out five oranges, three stamps and so on from the things he is selling. A till, with some real

Playing "store" has enormous appeal for children, especially if you have saved some empty boxes for them to "sell." It is a game that encourages your child to count as well as to engage in polite conversation with the "customer."

money in it, makes the game even more realistic.

Memory games

Children often enjoy "Pairs" from an early age. Spread an ordinary deck of cards or cards especially designed for the purpose face down on the floor. Turn them up and, when you find a matching pair, you keep them; if they don't match you turn them face down again in the same place. The one with the most pairs wins. Most parents are amazed to find that once they have got the hang of it, their child remembers as well as or even better than they do. In addition to encouraging his memory, playing Pairs helps him to concentrate and to recognize matching sets, both useful pre-reading skills.

Another memory game you can play together is to put four or five familiar objects on a tray. Let him look at them for a minute or so, then take the tray away and see how many he remembers. To vary the game, let him study the tray, then turn away while you remove one object. He then has to work out what's missing.

Recognizing letters

Memory and recognition play a large part in learning letters too. From looking at books with you and watching you read, your child becomes aware of letters, then starts to see how they are used.

Board games help to develop social skills like cooperation and turn-taking.

You can help make learning letters fun by making an alphabet scrapbook. Write each letter boldly at the top of the page and look together in old magazines, postcards, calendars and so on for pictures of objects beginning with that letter to stick in, perhaps writing the word in underneath.

Depending on the pace of your child's development, and the degree of pleasure he gets from letter sounds and playing with letters, your child may enjoy alphabet jigsaws, with a picture next to its corresponding letter, word jigsaws and an alphabet and number tray where letters and numbers fit into their own wells. Magnetic letters and numbers that stick to the fridge are also fun and can be in easy reach for your child to play with. Using these magnetic letters, you can make an alphabet lotto game. Trace the letters on to a large sheet of paper, divided into 26 squares and color them in. Your child can then place the magnetic letter over the matching square on the paper and get used to all the shapes of the letters. They

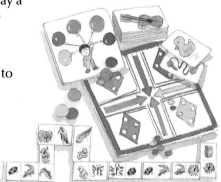

Making a card or present for someone else helps a child to learn the pleasure of giving.

don't have to be in alphabetical order and, in fact, might be more interesting to him if the letters of his name and other names and words he might be familiar with appear in order on the sheet.

Mailing a letter

With his new appreciation of the use of letters to make words your child may enjoy "writing" and mailing a letter to his granny, grandad or a favorite friend. He can draw a picture or write his name and put the paper in an envelope, which you address. He can stick on the stamp and mail it, or deliver it by hand. It may also be a way to encourage your child's social skills by writing a thank you "note" for a present or treat.

Books, stories and songs

The best start your child can have to learning to read is an appreciation of books as sources of pleasure and enjoyment.

During all the time they are growing up, but particularly in these years, children love to have "special" time when you are totally available to them. At this age it need only be 15 or 20 minutes a day and can be spent playing together, or just talking. Not only do your child's language skills improve with this sort of contact but also your understanding of your child and relationship with him will benefit enormously. Sometimes, this special time can be spent reading together. As your child grows, his taste in books will grow and change too. He will now be interested in more than just pictures; he will want to know the story.

A number of books are written for children to help prepare them for major changes or events in their lives, like going to playgroup, starting school, visiting an elderly relative, going into the hospital or the arrival of a new baby in the family. These, or stories that you make up yourself, told before the event, can help prepare him for what is going to happen and also give him an opportunity to say what he thinks about it. You can use stories too, to help your child overcome particular fears. If he's afraid of spiders or snakes, you could tell a story about a friendly one who comes to the rescue of a small child or who is seen to be defenseless and vulnerable, too.

Fairy tales
At this age, fairy stories are still popular, despite the fact that some parents fear that they are too frightening or grisly, especially in the original versions. However, it may be that fairy stories told in a secure environment actually help a child to overcome his fears of terrible things happening to him. Or he may feel so far removed from the characters that their experiences don't worry him because they are so unreal. Decide how much your child can tolerate and give him opportunities to talk about the story, answering his questions with care and understanding. And remember, in most fairy tales, everyone lives happily

ever after – a reassuring conclusion to point out if your child is worried by a story.

First reading

Your child may now begin to take an interest in words and reading himself. There are many books available that help to develop pre-reading skills, with activities teaching sequences, ordering, shape recognition and matching.

Simple reading books, some with a fuller version of the story for the adult to read and simple sentences in large letters on the other page for the child to read are also available. You can read these with your child, moving your finger over the words to show him that you read from left to right. When he knows the story, you can pause for him to supply a word, pointing to it with your finger, to get him used to the idea that a word of this shape and those letters has a certain sound and meaning. Your child may respond well to such gentle attempts to guide him towards reading while anything more obvious could put him off reading completely. Be guided by your child and the interest he shows in learning to read.

Here is a song to sing together

Miss Polly had a dolly who was sick, sick, sick,
So she sent for the doctor to come quick, quick, quick,
The doctor came with his bag and his hat
And he knocked on the door with a rat-tat-tat.
He looked at the dolly and he shook his head
And he said, "Miss Polly, put her straight to bed."
He wrote out a paper for a pill, pill, pill,
"I'll be back in the morning with my bill, bill, bill."

Mime rocking the doll, phoning the doctor, the hat and bag, knocking at the door, shaking the head, putting dolly in bed, and writing out a prescription. Five Currant Buns; The Mulberry Bush; and "London Bridge" are other favorites.

Listening skills

At this age it is very important just to encourage your child to listen to stories. He will particularly enjoy those you've made up about things that have happened to him and people he knows. You can encourage him to join in too by sometimes asking him what he thinks might happen next. This encourages him to listen and concentrate on the story as well as to think about the possible outcome.

Occasionally he may interrupt, saying, "No, I think he'd do such-and-such." Encourage him all you can to develop his imagination and his skills in putting ideas into words.

It can be fun to write down some of these favorite stories, too, asking your child to do the illustrations. These home-made books can be favorites for a while and then kept as mementoes to be looked at and enjoyed again and again.

Songs and nursery rhymes still have an important role in his life. If he can sing "Little Bo Peep," or "Row, row, row your boat" on his own, it can be fun trying it out as a round now with other children. It's exciting too, using percussion instruments to accompany a favorite tune.

Your child may enjoy especially playing musical games and singing songs with other children.

Active games

Physical games, indoors and out, are vital for developing your child's coordination and strength and for letting off steam. Your child may now be capable of a lot more activities; climbing to quite a height, jumping off higher and higher objects without falling, beginning to propel himself on a swing and being able to hop. Although he still needs supervision, he may be better able to judge his own abilities and limitations.

Children love going to a park or playground to use all the equipment they offer. They can also use jungle gyms and other structures for imaginative games, scaling a fortress or launching a spaceship from the top of the slide. If you are in the country or a wooded area, a real tree to climb is very exciting, and different altogether from a metal climbing frame. Children of this age need careful supervision, though, so that their play doesn't get out of hand and lead to an accident. A good outdoor game you can play with your child, or with a group, is to place two sticks on the ground, parallel to each other and about 1–2in (2–3cm) apart. Each child takes it in turn to jump over the sticks. Widen the gap and see if the children can still jump across.

Pedal power
If your child has had a tricycle, he may have scooted along using his feet to push himself. At about the age of three he may learn to pedal a trike. This requires coordination of his whole body, as well as balance and the physical strength to push the pedals. When he outgrows his trike he can progress to a small bicycle with training wheels. Buy one as large as he can comfortably manage, preferably with an adjustable seat and handlebars so that the pedal height is right and he will get the maximum use from it. Fit the training wheels so they stop the bicycle from wobbling at first; as your child gets older you can remove them when he has learned to balance.

He will need a firm, flat surface to practice riding on

Give your child every opportunity to visit a playground with its jungle gyms, slides, swings, seesaws and other equipment. These extend physical skills and increase self confidence – as well as being good fun.

Many children who were previously frightened of the water enjoy swimming as they get older and more confident.

and usually this can only be the pavement or a local playground. If your child goes out on the pavement, you will obviously need to be with him all the time. It's worth trying to incorporate bicycle-riding into a trip to the local shop or an outing to the park to give him lots of opportunity to practice and gain confidence.

Swimming

Swimming is splendid for pre-school children. Some groups run special 'waterbabies' classes meant to build up your child's confidence. By three or four, he may be able to swim by himself, equipped with water wings and/or an inner tube, but he still needs you near him. Children get quite alarmed if they go under and swallow some water and you're not there to provide instant help. You also need to make sure that an over-confident child doesn't go out of his depth.

Ball games

Ball games are more of a feature at this age too. A child may enjoy kicking a football about; he may also like to wield a small baseball bat or tennis racket. Hitting a ball with a bat isn't easy and you need to stand in close and provide lots of encouragement to help your child develop the necessary hand-to-eye coordination.

Throwing and catching are tricky for pre-school children. However, if your child is at the right stage of development, then practice helps the skills to improve. Start with a big ball for catching and don't throw it hard enough to hurt if he catches it awkwardly on the ends of his fingers. A small bean bag, which gives a better grip than a ball, is excellent for this first catching practice. You might consider making your own from a small rectangle of sturdy cloth, folded in half, stitched on three sides, filled with small dried beans, and sewn closed. The stitching need not be perfect as long as it holds.

Throwing is also practiced by playing hoop-la with a peg board and small rubber rings.

Your child will love racing around with you, in the park, along a beach or in the garden. He may also enjoy simple obstacle races, just testing his own ability to complete the course, perhaps with a given time limit – say, by the time you have counted to 50. An egg-and-spoon race (or potato or stone-and-spoon) or hopping race is popular too.

Walking along a log or low wall, putting one foot in front of the other, is a skill that your child may perfect at this age.

Your child's progress

Once your child reaches the age of three, his development seems more subtle and less dramatic. However, he is learning all the time and needs to play and experiment with a growing variety of toys and games to build on the skills which have gone before and to develop new ones. Books, paints, construction toys and games involving other children become more and more important as his knowledge and understanding grow.

Control of his body
He learns to balance on a narrow surface and can also hop. His hands and arms can take his weight, enabling him to swing from a bar or pull himself up with his hands. From the age of three your child may be able to pedal a tricycle and by five to cycle some distance. If he has confidence in the water, he may be able to swim unaided or with an inner tube.

Control of his hands
Your child's hands become stronger and steadier and he is able to carry out sustained movements such as to cut with scissors, put things together and draw with increasing skill. By five he may be able to draw a clear picture, write the letters of his name and may set out to make something, rather than labelling it when he is finished.

Talking and understanding
Your child's speech develops at a great rate as he learns to put more complex sentences together and express his thoughts more accurately. He learns the right order for words and gradually learns the rules of language through repetition. He asks questions constantly using "why," "what" and "how" and he may make up rhymes and stories too.

Social skills
At five your child may be quite independent and may enjoy playing in his own room or space, needing much less adult involvement in his activities. He may have special friends and playmates and can play cooperatively, sharing and taking turns. He also forms close relationships with relatives and other adults he sees often.

Thinking and planning ahead
Between three and five your child's ability to think ahead and see where his actions will lead him becomes more developed. He can play simple games which involve thinking out what happens next. He may improve his sense of time and be able to wait and plan for events. He may be more willing to accept a change in activity if you warn him in advance.

Top twenty toys

Through play – and the toys that encourage it – a child learns to think and explore, develops physical skills, gains confidence and starts to communicate and be sociable.
The toys suggested here have been chosen because they are the ones that give a child a great deal of enjoyment as well as learning potential from birth to five years. They cover a wide range of activities and provide a core to promote the development of all your child's basic skills. If they are well made and durable they should give your child considerable satisfaction for a long time.
Avoid toys made of brittle plastic or those that are too fragile. Toys that break easily are frustrating, at best, and at worst, dangerous. Toys may be played with then left, to be returned to later when they may be used in new and different ways.

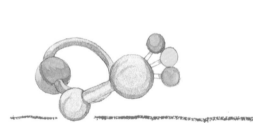

Rattles
Rattles come in a wide variety of sizes: look for those which are easy to hold, make a satisfying noise, have moving parts and are comfortable for your baby to chew or suck. They are the first noise-making toy, attracting attention and encouraging your child to reach, grasp, improve his hand/ eye coordination and start to learn about cause and effect. Later on they can be used as rhythm instruments to play along in musical games.

Soft toys
A well-chosen soft toy will delight your baby early on as you brush it against her skin or tickle it on her tummy. It can provide a familiar object to help her feel secure at bedtime and later may be involved in your child's games and early attempts at conversation. It may become a playmate she talks to and confides in, encouraging communication and language skills.

Activity center
An activity center begins to interest your baby at around six months of age and may continue to fascinate until he is 18 months or more. Most have a variety of knobs and buttons that require different hand and finger movements to operate them: turning, spinning, poking or flicking. He acquires these one by one and practices using them. Most are designed to attach to the side of a crib or playpen, or can be played with on the floor.

Telephone
A toy telephone is an invaluable toy from the age of six months. At first your child enjoys twiddling the dial (or pressing the buttons) and taking the receiver on and off. As she gets older she will carry on pretend conversations and seem to listen, encouraging the development of communication skills, and may incorporate the telephone into other make-believe games.

Stacking cups
Stacking cups exercise a number of your child's skills; he can bang them together, fit them inside one another, build towers with them, knock them down, hide things under them, sort them into colors and use them as containers for pretend play or for play with water or sand. Look for those which contain at least ten to a set. Some stacking cups have small and large holes in the bases of some of the cups, to use in sand and water.

Shape sorter
Shape sorters vary from a simple mailbox with holes into which different shapes fit, to elaborate containers with many complex shapes. The simple ones are better for younger babies, but the more complex will still be testing a child of two years and beyond, encouraging hand skills, matching and discrimination as well as helping to make a child aware that objects that "disappear" still exist.

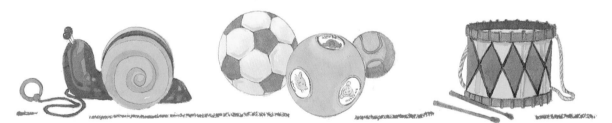

Pull-along toy
A pull-along toy can be useful at first for a sitting baby. Once your child is steady on her feet a pull-along encourages coordination and balance as she keeps looking back over her shoulder and uses one hand to pull the toy. Pull-alongs that are stable and make a satisfying noise or move in an interesting way as they are pulled give the most enjoyment. They require fine finger movements to hold the string and pull it.

Balls
A crawling baby will love chasing after a ball for the sheer fun of it, a toddler rolling it and trying to catch it, and an older child kicking, throwing and playing organized games. A small plastic one with holes can be held in one hand by a baby. A large inflatable beach ball or a soft ball is good for two-handed play and a robust ball is ideal for kicking. Ball games also encourage social skills such as interaction, communication and turn-taking.

"Music" toy
Small children love music and musical toys provide great pleasure. A baby can listen to a music box perhaps operating it himself as he gets older. Instruments like a xylophone or drum can be used as banging toys, then as rhythm and tune makers. Playing instruments encourages listening and copying, so he needs to use his memory, and is also a good social activity, encouraging cooperation and turn-taking.

Books

Books of all kinds are of interest to your child. From an early age she associates them with close contact with you – sitting on your lap and hearing your voice. Start with simple cloth and board books, progressing to those with flaps which open to reveal pictures underneath and then to those with more complex pictures. These help build vocabulary and communication skills. Books that tell a story stimulate her memory and imagination.

Pushcart – and blocks

A pushcart helps your child gain confidence in walking and may later have other uses too. He may enjoy taking dolls for a ride in it or transporting his toys, using the cart as an accessory in pretend play later. Choose one which is sturdy and will not tip up easily when he puts his full weight on the handle. Blocks are an essential first building toy to help him develop his manipulative skills and dexterity.

Sit-and-ride toy

Children love the freedom of mobility they get when they push themselves along on a sit-and-ride toy, on which they can scoot about inside and outdoors. A sit-and-ride toy may well get constant use from 18 months to four years or more. It improves balance and integrates arm, leg and body movements, as well as encouraging your child to plan where she is going and work out how to get out of a tight spot if she gets stuck.

Tea set

A tea set is a wonderful "let's pretend" toy as it encourages imitative play, then stimulates your child's imagination, use of language and understanding. A strong, simple set with teapot, cups and saucers, a milk pitcher, sugar bowl and spoon will be enough for most play. A teapot is also good for pouring games in the bath or for watering plants in the garden.

Dolls

Boys and girls both enjoy a doll, especially one which is strong, simple and well-made, either from plastic or fabric. A lifesize newborn doll can be dressed in outgrown baby clothes adding to its realism which children love. A doll is talked to, encouraging speech development, cuddled, giving a child an outlet for her feelings, and central to "let's pretend" play. Some children like a rag doll they can clutch, others prefer a realistic one.

Puzzles

Puzzles help your child with visual coordination and recognition of shapes and patterns. They give practice at problem-solving, encourage planning with a goal in mind and require concentration. The first to introduce are inset boards or playtrays, then those where a small number of pieces fit into a board. Floor puzzles with big pieces can usually be coped with next and finally jigsaws with more and more pieces.

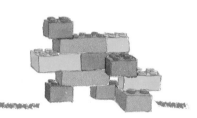

Modelling materials

Playdough or clay provides your child with a medium which is a new means of creative expression for her. She can squeeze it, poke it, pat and make shapes with it at first, enjoying the experience of using her hands in a new and different way. Then she may make representations of cakes, cars and other simple models. A small rolling pin, shapes for cutting out and perhaps molds may all be used to add to her enjoyment.

Crayons, pens and chalk

Drawing is at first an imitative activity which helps to improve eye–hand coordination and dexterity, then a creative activity for your child, who needs crayons and pens which fit his age and skills. Start him off with short, chunky non-toxic wax crayons and progress to washable felt tips, colored pencils and chalks. Drawing enables him to begin using skills such as making patterns and copying shapes which are needed for later writing.

Construction toy

A good construction toy that is sturdy, strong and can be added to and adapted as your child grows provides many play opportunities. As well as needing the skillful use of two hands, your child's creativity and planning and problem-solving abilities are exercised. The pieces should fit together firmly but not be too hard to pull apart or too small for a young child. Some come with small people, farm animals and other miniatures.

Practical toy

A toy such as a tool kit, a threading set or lacing cards that enables a child to do something he has seen you do is attractive for its imitative qualities but also encourages him to carry out actions that improve fine finger or hand movements, that require the use of two hands working together and good hand–eye coordination. Such toys improve concentration and problem-solving abilities and require sustained effort.

Miniature toys

Many children are fascinated by miniature figures with which they can act out make-believe games. These include the dolls and furniture in a doll's house, farm and zoo animals, the figures which fit into a garage set or train layout, or figures of firemen, cowboys and Indians, spacemen, doctors and nurses, and the like. Toy cars may be included here. Some of these figures have tiny props which are unsafe for under threes.

Toy storage

* Storing toys neatly makes your home safer since 50% of accidents involving toys occur because someone has fallen over them

* Toys can be stored in an open toy box, stacking storage boxes, a wicker basket, or a toy chest

* Keep jigsaws and toys with small pieces in containers with lids so the pieces don't get lost

* Toys that need supervision should be stored out of reach

* Store toys where your child can get to them, to choose what he wants to play with, and also where he can help to put them away.

TOYS AND SAFETY

To be safe, toys should be well-made, able to withstand heavy use, even in ways for which they were not designed, suitable for the child's age and made of non-toxic materials. A smaller collection of well-made toys from reliable manufacturers may cost more than a lot of cheaper, badly-made toys but is a safer option and the toys should last longer.

Ask your pediatrician about safety guidelines for your child's toys, games and activities.

Safe toys at the right age

Check the age guide on the packet. Although many toys are safe for children younger than the ages given, the package should say if the toy is unsuitable for a younger child. Many toys designed for older children can be harmful for babies and younger children, especially when they are at the stage of putting everything into their mouths. Be particularly careful of soft, jelly-like toys, often shaped like dinosaurs or monsters. They can harden and become sharp and dangerous if chewed or swallowed when the plasticizer that is added to

soften them has been dissolved in a baby's mouth or stomach. Even paints and crayons labelled non-toxic may be harmful if eaten in large quantities.

Some dolls or soft toys from which the eyes, nose or other parts can fall off are unsafe because the small bits can be swallowed and may leave behind sharp hooks or spikes. If a toy has hair that can be pulled out, this may be swallowed or cause a small child to choke. These problems should not arise if toys are bought from a reputable shop or retailer, but you should be especially wary of toys from market stalls or cheap trinkets sold at holiday time.

Toys with tiny pieces, marbles, small dice, counters and markers and toys with tiny batteries should all be kept out of a baby's reach. These objects can be swallowed or cause children to choke. For these reasons, any object which is less than 1½in (4cm) in any dimension should be kept away from babies and young toddlers. Watch out, too, for toys with strings attached which can be swallowed or

become wrapped around a baby's neck.

Be careful of glues. Never let your child use any "instant" glues or those which give off harmful vapors. The best to use is polyvinyl acetate (PVA) glue which is non-toxic, washes out with cold water and is useful for most sticking.

Supervision of play and toys

Remember that your children need supervision in many activities especially if you have younger and older children playing together. Many accidents causing injury happen because toys are thrown. Keep an older child's toys away from a younger child by storing them out of reach.

When toys get broken they may no longer be safe. If they cannot be mended it is best to throw them away. Be careful if you buy a second-hand toy – make sure it is not broken or damaged. Be aware that it might have been made prior to the toy safety regulations.

If a toy is battery-operated, ask the shopkeeper if it is safe if the batteries are accidentally inserted the wrong way.

Index

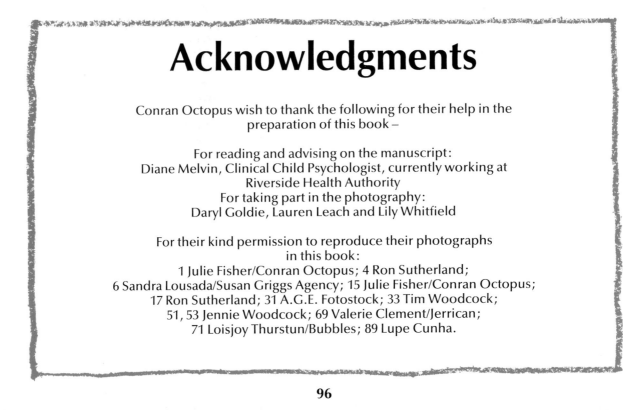

Acknowledgments

Conran Octopus wish to thank the following for their help in the preparation of this book –

For reading and advising on the manuscript:
Diane Melvin, Clinical Child Psychologist, currently working at Riverside Health Authority
For taking part in the photography:
Daryl Goldie, Lauren Leach and Lily Whitfield

For their kind permission to reproduce their photographs in this book:
1 Julie Fisher/Conran Octopus; 4 Ron Sutherland;
6 Sandra Lousada/Susan Griggs Agency; 15 Julie Fisher/Conran Octopus;
17 Ron Sutherland; 31 A.G.E. Fotostock; 33 Tim Woodcock;
51, 53 Jennie Woodcock; 69 Valerie Clement/Jerrican;
71 Loisjoy Thurstun/Bubbles; 89 Lupe Cunha.